AVID
READER
PRESS

IN A WORLD OF SUNRISES

365 DAYS OF HEART, SOUL, AND HOPE

CLEO WADE

AVID READER PRESS

NEW YORK AMSTERDAM/ANTWERP LONDON
TORONTO SYDNEY/MELBOURNE NEW DELHI

Avid Reader Press
An Imprint of Simon & Schuster, LLC
1230 Avenue of the Americas
New York, NY 10020

First Avid Reader Press hardcover edition April 2026

AVID READER PRESS and colophon are trademarks of Simon & Schuster, LLC

Manufactured in the United States of America

1 3 5 7 9 10 8 6 4 2

Library of Congress Control Number: 2025945121

ISBN 978-1-6682-1071-0
ISBN 978-1-6682-1073-4 (ebook)

For my sunshine girls—

Memphis, Bayou & Magnolia

Dearest You,

In a World of Sunrises is a collection of poems and ideas created to ground us in what's important: Heart. Soul. And Hope.

The center of your heart is where peace and gratitude reside. When we stay connected to this loving lifeline, we make better choices for ourselves, we have more clarity, and we have access to our center, no matter how dizzying the world around us feels.

To live with soul is to remember that spirituality includes life's pleasures. Soul is the birthplace of joy—it breeds belly laughs, friendship, music, dancing, art of all mediums, and the perfect bite of food. It is the magic. The pixie dust. The good stuff.

Hope is how we keep going. The world has always been filled to the brim with beauty and tragedy. Hope reminds us that we are worth it. We are worth the extra mile, the sleepless nights, the nerve and the bravery it takes to speak truth to power. It keeps us feisty and resilient and links us to something bigger than ourselves.

As with all of my work, this book is intended to be lived with, dog-eared, written on, and shared with loved ones. Maybe you read a page each day with your morning coffee. Maybe you keep it in your bag in case you need a pick-me-up throughout the day. Or maybe it sits next to a glass of water on your nightstand. However it shows up in your precious life, I pray it is useful and brings a small moment of happiness or serenity whenever you need one.

DAY 1.

TRUSTING YOUR PATH HELPS YOU MAKE SENSE OF WHAT YOU ENCOUNTER ALONG THE WAY.

Each morning, try saying to yourself: *I trust where I am going. I trust that everything on my path is here for me to love, learn from, or meet with grace.* When we don't have trust, we add a layer of discomfort to every experience and relationship in our lives. Second-guessing everything is a manifestation of fear. It burns our energy and keeps us running in place. Trust is born from bravery; it moves us forward.

DAY 2.

GETTING HONEST IS LIKE
PUTTING THE WINDSHIELD
WIPERS ON IN HEAVY RAIN—
WE BEGIN TO SEE EVERYTHING
AROUND US MORE CLEARLY.
IT IS MUCH EASIER TO FIGURE
OUT WHERE YOU WANT TO GO
WHEN YOU CAN TRULY SEE
WHERE YOU ARE RIGHT NOW.

DAY 3.

Many of us struggle to create boundaries because we do not feel worthy of comfort. Since society often praises self-sacrifice and over-accommodation, we might even feel special because of our ability to deal with discomfort. Self-worth helps us establish boundaries. We must believe we are deserving of consideration in order to advocate for it. Know that your wants, desires, and needs belong in all of your important relationships. Know that your safety and comfort belong in every room you enter.

DAY 4.

more of this

when is the last time
you danced your heart out
alone at home or in the middle of the dance floor?
when is the last time
you took your shoes off and ran in a field for no good reason?
more of this
more moments of simple freedom
more vacations from the opinions of everybody else

DAY 5.

We must get to know ourselves and learn how to enjoy who we are before we ask anyone else to. This is the only way we can have relationships that feel easeful and do not burden others with problems that are not theirs to solve. Usually, when we feel like someone is "work," it is because they are requesting that we be responsible for their happiness or the state of their self-esteem. Of course, we must be kind to one another and nurture those we love, and each of us must have a firm understanding of what is *me work* and what is *we work*.

DAY 6.

COMPARISON IS OFTEN A FORM OF PROCRASTINATION—WE WASTE TIME LOOKING OVER OUR NEIGHBOR'S FENCE INSTEAD OF TENDING TO OUR OWN GARDEN. ALLOW YOUR OBSERVATIONS OF OTHERS TO BE BRIEF, PURPOSEFUL, AND POSITIVE SO YOU CAN STAY FOCUSED ON AND GRATEFUL FOR YOUR OWN PATH.

DAY 7.

The mind holds so much information. It can sometimes feel like the drawer in the house where you stuff all the things you don't want to throw out—pictures, notes, holiday cards, bills, reminders. Even though we put off cleaning it out, it always feels good once we do. When was the last time you wrote down your thoughts? Self-examination helps us to better understand and organize our dreams, desires, and hopes for our lives. It also gives us an opportunity to see what may be blocking or bothering us. Empty the drawer. Take note of every idea, worry, person, conflict, and happy-making thought that crosses your consciousness.

DAY 8.

SOME OBSTACLES ARE MEANT TO BE TACKLED, SOME ARE MEANT TO BE WALKED AROUND, AND SOME ARE MEANT TO BE PUT IN A LITTLE BOAT AND PUSHED OUT TO SEA. DO WHAT FEELS RIGHT FOR YOU. THERE IS NOT ONE RIGHT WAY TO MOVE THROUGH OR MOVE ON FROM OUR DIFFICULTIES.

DAY 9.

Manifestation is not a genie granting a wish or a thought that magically becomes reality without effort. It is the practice of visualizing yourself at your finish line as you work toward it. It is the steadfast belief that you will reach your destination no matter what comes up. This mindset will always move you closer to having what is in your heart. It certainly will never lead you farther away.

DAY 10.

WHAT DOES A GOOD DAY FEEL LIKE?

WHAT DO YOU SEE? SMELL? HEAR? ARE YOU ALONE? WITH OTHERS? IS THE SUN OUT? IS THE MOON?

* IT IS EASIER TO FIND SOMETHING WHEN YOU KNOW WHAT YOU ARE LOOKING FOR.

DAY 11.

We experience burnout when we ignore our needs for extended periods of time and prioritize external stressors over internal harmony. When we find ourselves more committed to what fatigues, strains, or dulls us—from phone scrolling to overworking—it eventually removes us from our center. We feel irritable, unmotivated, and down. Finding a sense of calm and okay-ness is possible, even in today's fast-paced world, but it requires us to invest in restorative activities and set boundaries with what drains our energy.

DAY 12.

I have always loved the saying "all in good time." Time is not always the enemy. Time can be good to us, especially when we are not trying to outsmart it or obsessively control it. We do not need to rush through our artistic and personal processes, precious moments, or phases of life. Our lives unfold in their own divine way. All in good time.

DAY 13.

DREAMS ARE NOT MEANT TO LIE DORMANT. TO DREAM IS TO REBEL. PEOPLE MAY TELL US TO "GET REAL" OR "BE PRACTICAL," BUT OUR DREAMS REMIND US THAT THERE IS SOMETHING MAGICAL INSIDE OF US. EACH ONE OF US HAS A SPARKLING LIGHT YEARNING TO SHINE IN ITS OWN SPECIAL WAY.

DAY 14.

Anxiety is when worry is the loudest voice in your head. But like a baby screaming, it can be soothed by calm, consistent, comforting affirmation: *It is okay, it is okay, it is okay.* Next, we can gently ask ourselves, what could help? What need is unmet? Breath? Water? Food? Support? A soft and slow approach to a tough moment is often more constructive than a harsh one.

DAY 15.

rich

rich is
I woke up and everything in this body worked (for the most part)
rich is
summertime and peaches are in season
rich is
"okay, talk to you later. I love you, bye"
rich is
"here, have some of mine" and "let me help you with that"
rich is
free concerts in the park, sandwiches, and the secret wine we share in our paper cups
it's sleeping late on a rainy morning, it's snuggles, it's coffee, it's leftovers that taste better the next day
rich is
"just calling to say I made it home safe"
"okay, I love you, bye"

DAY 16.

Michael Jordan was cut from his varsity high school basketball team. It is said Walt Disney was fired from his job at the local newspaper because he "lacked imagination and had no good ideas." No one has the power to tell us who we are unless we value their opinion more than our own. Our destiny is not in the hands of others, nor can it be dictated by perceived failures. We must always try and try again because even if we know where we want to go, we never know how or when we will get there.

DAY 17.

JUST AS AN ALCHEMIST CAN TURN LEAD INTO GOLD, WE CAN ALLOW LOVE AND PATIENCE TO BRING NEW MEANING TO OUR DIFFICULTIES. WE CAN TRANSFORM OUR STRUGGLES, WE CAN EVEN TURN THEM INTO STRENGTHS.

DAY 18.

What would our lives look like without blame? We often get caught up in the stories we tell ourselves. When we are upset, we quickly begin casting the villain, hero, and victim. What does reality look like when we drop these roles? Each of us is a mix of nerves, feelings, gifts, attractions, and triggers, with shadow and light constantly dancing within. When we accept this truth, we are less likely to point the finger in conflict. Removing emotionally charged narratives or drama allows us to accurately assess behaviors and focus on what's relevant. From there, we can do the next best thing for ourselves, whether that be space for reflection, a conversation toward resolution, or a considered exit.

DAY 19.

recipe for oneness

I want for you
what I want for me
I want for your loved ones
what I want for mine
love, safety, bellies filled with food and laughter
a place we call home with pride and joy
oh, what a world we could give to each other

DAY 20.

The ego is terribly unreliable. Most of the time, it processes our experiences in hollow half-truths. If we rely on it to inform our decisions, it usually leads us into toxic behavior, isolation, or bad company. The ego makes us feel everyone is against us, obsessed with us, or in competition with us. The truth is most people have a very full plate, and don't have the time or energy to think about us too much. Spirit recognizes this, and encourages us to simply be kind, do our best, and want the best for others.

DAY 21.

Family can look however we want it to look. It does not need to be limited to family of origin or childbirth. Belonging, kinship, and parenting come in many forms. We are allowed to create a life centered on *what feels like family* rather than reaching for a picture of what family should be according to some. When we do this, we can find fulfillment in the unique quality of our chosen relationships. Happiness more often comes from creating a path of our own, not from following one prescribed by society or someone else.

DAY 22.

Life is messy. Emotions are messy. In that muddiness, mistakes happen. Our character is defined by what we do next. Do we hold ourselves accountable after we take a harsh tone with someone, or do we blame them? Do we offer repair to those hurt by our actions? Do we expect an emotional hall pass because something was an accident? Making mistakes is human. Making amends and taking responsibility for ourselves is being a grown-up.

DAY 23.

DETOURS ARE SIGNS TOO. JUST BECAUSE A SIGN IS INCONVENIENT DOES NOT MEAN IT IS WRONG OR INSIGNIFICANT. DETOURS CAN OFTEN LEAD US TO NEEDED LESSONS, EXPERIENCES, AND NEW PEOPLE WE WOULD HAVE OTHERWISE MISSED. DIVINE TIMING IS REAL (AND INCLUDES OUR PERCEIVED DELAYS).

DAY 24.

LETTING GO IS A DECISION AND A PRACTICE.

When something is stuck on a loop in your mind, it helps to create a practice of letting it go. This may look like a long walk, repeating the words, *I am letting this go with every step.* Or during a shower, bath, or swim in the ocean, repeating the words, *I am allowing the water to wash this experience away from me.* When we truly want to let go of a situation, we are willing to rewire not only how we think about it but how often we think about it. Only you can pause the loop in order to move on.

DAY 25.

When we benefit from other people's time and support, it is important to be gracious and recognize their efforts and contributions. No one wants to feel invisible. We all want to feel loved, seen, and held. Gratitude sustains our relationships, it is a healthy offering and request.

DAY 26.

"I've been absolutely terrified every moment of my life, and I've never let it keep me from doing a single thing I wanted to do."

—Georgia O'Keeffe

We are all afraid. It helps to know that. People everywhere are falling in love, chasing dreams, taking risks, inventing, and creating. And they are doing it all scared. When we realize this, we begin seeing inspiration for living a brave life all around us.

DAY 27.

Acclaimed actor Daniel Day-Lewis won three Academy Awards and left Hollywood for many years to become a shoemaker in Italy. Sometimes we must walk away from one dream to pursue another. As Walt Whitman said, we "contain multitudes." There are many worlds within us yearning to be expressed and explored.

DAY 28.

what love is

love is not "I want you."
love is "I'm here for you."
it holds near without ownership
it receives from the other without robbing the other
it offers the self without draining the self
like the sun and the moon
its light shares, reflects, and dances in natural harmony.

DAY 29.

"The longer I live, the more deeply I learn that love—whether we call it friendship or family or romance—is the work of mirroring and magnifying each other's light."

—James Baldwin

Love is the divine sharing of all that we are. Not always easy, but always worth it.

DAY 30.

WE CANNOT LIVE OUR LIVES IN ARMOR. STRENGTH CAN BE SOFT, OPEN, AND HONEST. TO AVOID VULNERABILITY IS TO AVOID POSSIBILITY.

DAY 31.

We live *with* grief. We live with the memories. We live with the love. We live with the loss. This is why grief requires grace. Grace is the place where love meets patience. It replaces judgment with care and doesn't believe our emotions have expiration dates. We may feel different shades of healing, and the pain may shift, but we walk alongside our grief for the rest of our lives. We must allow grace to follow along.

DAY 32.

Life is often a mirror—reflective of the mood we offer it. When we only see life for its ability to humble, test, or teach tough lessons, we miss out on the beautiful friendship and support it can also offer. We stand on a planet spinning in space, and life is here: holding us, making it possible for us to dream, love, and be. This does not mean we live in the delusion that life is without hardship; it means we feel the hope and kinship it also offers. To see life as a friend is to look in the mirror with a smile.

DAY 33.

OTHER PEOPLE DO NOT NEED TO LIKE YOU IN ORDER FOR YOU TO LIKE YOURSELF. (EVEN THE ONES YOU REALLY WANT TO LIKE YOU.) YOU ARE THE ONE WHO DECIDES THAT YOU ARE WORTHY, LIKABLE, AND LOVABLE.

DAY 34.

Day and night, there is a voice within whispering your feelings, dreams, and new ideas. Often, it gets drowned out by the constant stream of media and personalities we engage with, but the more we listen to ourselves, the louder and clearer our inner voice becomes. It strengthens our relationship to ourselves and connects us more deeply to our wisdom within.

DAY 35.

We are all walking around with scars. Some visible, some invisible. May this thought alone be the reason we are gentle with ourselves and others. We really don't know the depth of other people's pain. When we feel someone is unfairly lashing out at us, we do not have to excuse their behavior, nor do we need to create a narrative that they are the worst person on earth. We can have our feelings, give grace, and, if needed, give space. We can remember that people are often reacting from old, deep wounds.

DAY 36.

DARK TIMES REQUIRE DEEP IMAGINATION.

We must never underestimate the power of our imagination. Our hardships need wild ideas. Creative thought is something no one can take from you. As long as you are alive, you have an imagination that can wrap the world's problems in incredible art or extraordinarily loving solutions. Your imagination is an infinite, natural resource. When you can tap into it, it flows in plenty.

DAY 37.

altogether known

I say nothing
you say nothing
your eyes meet mine
laughter erupts
a long story made short with one glance
this is the language
of friends
mischievous and divine every time

DAY 38.

CLARITY GIFTS US CALM IN THE CENTER OF OUR STORMS.

Clarity is the starting point for healing. Before we try to escape an unwanted feeling or situation, we must wholly identify it. We must know the location and severity of our wound in order to heal it. We must quiet the noise and rise above our situation (if only for a moment). From there, we better understand what we need to do next. We see more clearly what or who can support us through our tough time.

DAY 39.

We choose most of our thoughts, all of our words, and much of the company we keep. We choose whether we heal or cause harm. We choose kindness or cruelty, selfishness or generosity, building or destroying. Our choices are sacred, serious business. It is never too late to take responsibility for your life by owning your choices.

DAY 40.

WE HONOR THE DREAM BY DOING THE WORK.

Many people came before us to make our rights, jobs, education, and other social and environmental privileges possible. Who you are, what you have, and who you get to love are dreams come true for those who came before you. Isn't that amazing? We can show gratitude for this epic ancestral gift by continuing their work toward a brighter future. It is deeply powerful to leave a beloved blueprint and radiant dream for the world to inherit.

DAY 41.

Love is unconditional. It is spiritual. It wraps around every wound—no matter the size or depth—without shame or otherness. Relationships, however, are conditional. They require shared agreements, responsibilities, and healthy expectations in order to flourish. Sometimes love and relationships flow seamlessly and sometimes they are in conflict. Know that you can always send and hold love for someone even if a relationship is no longer possible. The spiritual and the practical cannot always walk the same line. Accepting this truth allows us to honor both love and healthy boundaries.

DAY 42.

RIGHT NOW, YOU ARE ALIVE.
YOUR HEART IS BEATING.
THE EARTH IS HOLDING YOU
UP IN THE MIDDLE OF A
STARRY, ENDLESS UNIVERSE.
RIGHT NOW, YOU ARE HERE.
LET GRATITUDE FILL YOU
AND LEAD YOU TO YOUR
NEXT MOMENT. LIFE, EVEN
WITH ITS DIFFICULTIES,
IS ONE BIG MIRACLE.

DAY 43.

To find contentment—peace in our hearts, calm in our minds—we must have a relationship with enough-ness. What is enough? What is enough stuff? Money? Attention? More, more, more is an all-encompassing energy, that inevitably leaves us feeling exhausted and empty rather than grateful and satisfied. We must boundary this bottomless yearning so we can spend our lives in appreciation and generosity instead of thirst.

DAY 44.

ASK FOR HELP. GET HELP. BECOME A HELPER. THIS IS THE CIRCLE OF COMMUNITY. WE ALL NEED HELP AT SOME POINT; THERE IS NO SHAME IN THIS, AND THERE ARE MANY HELPERS WHO WERE ONCE IN YOUR SHOES. MAKE THE FIRST STEP. ASK. RECEIVE. PAY IT FORWARD.

DAY 45.

When was the last time you really thought about your breath? Someone once told me anxiety is breath moving too quickly and depression is breath moving too slowly. Our breath is profoundly powerful. Can't sleep? Breathe. Can't calm down? Breathe. Scared? Breathe. Hurt or upset? Breathe. Our breath deserves great respect and reverence. It gives us life and brings us back to center.

DAY 46.

Friendship is a shared bond and a social safety net. It can be a divine refuge from a world that can feel incredibly harsh. When seeking new friendships, first ask yourself, *What is the quality of friendship I offer?* We sometimes find ourselves searching for what we have not yet cultivated within. If we are yearning for a good listener, we must also know how to listen with patience and understanding. If we seek slow, undivided attention from others, we must be prepared to hold that same space for them. Healthy bonds are bidirectional—they flow both ways with ease. There are moments when one person may be centered, but no one should be constantly bending the dynamic in their direction.

DAY 47.

Violence has no home in our hearts. Harmful words and actions are manifestations of pain and unmet needs. When we feel the need to lash out, we must investigate what within us is hurting. We all have the power to veer heated emotions like anger and frustration away from toxic behavior toward light. Heat is energy. So is light. We must learn how to regulate and shape it so that our presence adds love to our communities instead of hate. A more peaceful world always begins with more peaceful people.

DAY 48.

SEEK JOY. SEE LIVE MUSIC. SING AND DANCE WITH STRANGERS. GO TO BALL GAMES, PARKS, AND LIBRARIES. MAKE ART. FIND ART—WHETHER IT IS IN MUSEUMS OR ON THE SIDE OF A BUILDING. EVEN IN MOMENTS OF DARKNESS, THERE ARE STILL LITTLE LIGHTS ALL AROUND US. FIND ONE TODAY. BE ONE TODAY.

DAY 49.

It is important to ask ourselves how we feel after we spend time with our close friends and family. These bonds have the power to lift, soothe, and re-center us. We must also take note of comments that dig at our self-esteem or foster self-doubt. The people we choose to share our lives with shouldn't be the same people who make us feel insecure. Good friends help us feel good about ourselves.

DAY 50.

on peace

when I say I come in peace
I mean my hands are open
prepared to hold your falling head, meet your rising hand, wrap around your open wound.
peace is an offering
if it cannot remove your pain
it will walk beside it tenderly

DAY 51.

Life is a big wow. It truly is. At least once a day, try to connect to awe. Notice the hugeness of the sky. See a bee float from flower to flower, watch a leaf glide toward the ground, whispering, *Fall is on the way*. We get very busy, move very quickly, and hold past experiences that become very heavy. Life feels like something that is constantly happening *to* us instead of *with and for* us. Today, take a minute to find awe. Let it reconnect you to the slow beauty of aliveness.

DAY 52.

Your mental real estate is valuable. Don't let anything and everything run wild in your mind or drain your light. One of the mantras I use most from *Heart Talk* is: **Remember not to care about the things you don't even care about**. It is a reminder that we can place internal boundaries on the space we allow trivial dramas to occupy.

DAY 53.

Is your pride in the way? Are you holding a grudge that is no longer important to you? Let go of what doesn't matter, especially if it is blocking your connection with others. We get so used to carrying around hurt feelings, we may not notice when they have mellowed or disappeared altogether. When something no longer really bothers you, let it go, move on, or reconnect. Most grudges have an expiration date.

DAY 54.

Through presence we can release the past. This does not erase yesterday's experiences—joyful or terrible—it just acknowledges that what happened is not *still* happening. We have a past for a reason—we cannot carry the weight of everything that has happened to us every day for the rest of our lives.

DAY 55.

We all want serenity. Perhaps this is why the serenity prayer is so enduring: *God, grant me the serenity to accept the things I cannot change, the courage to change the things I can, and the wisdom to know the difference.* These timeless words remind us that peace can be at the center of our existence no matter what we are going through. Peace is held in ease and tumult. It is held in stillness and in doingness.

DAY 56.

"Nothing happens until something moves."

—Albert Einstein

When we feel stuck or sad, we are often told to move on or move forward. But depending on what we are going through, that can feel impossible. Sometimes the best thing we can do is just . . . move. Not forward. Not backward. Just move our bodies. Part of why dancing feels so great is because there is no destination. We get to simply enjoy the benefits of moving energy through and around our being.

DAY 57.

OUR FEELINGS ARE IMPERMANENT. THIS CAN BE KIND OF SCARY AND ALSO KIND OF A RELIEF. THEY CAN SHIFT IN BIG WAYS OVER TIME OR EVER SO SLIGHTLY MINUTE TO MINUTE. LEAVE ROOM FOR YOUR EMOTIONAL TIDES TO CHANGE. WHAT HURTS CAN FADE INTO WHAT HEALS FASTER THAN YOU THINK.

DAY 58.

"To do two things at once is to do neither."

—Publilius Syrus

We are more productive and present when we focus on one thing at a time. Our relationships need presence and awareness to thrive. We cannot meaningfully connect with a loved one while we are working, driving, running errands, or scrolling through our phone. Resist the urge to make multitasking a way of life. It may give you quantity, but it will not give you quality.

DAY 59.

Our relationships ebb and flow based on where we are and what we are going through. Romantic and platonic relationships may last a lifetime or a summer. Our connections with family members may end after childhood or follow us into every phase of life. All of these relationships are ripe with valuable lessons that help us grow and better understand ourselves. There is wisdom in the old cliche "people come into your life for a season, a reason, or a lifetime." You are allowed to meet relational change with grace and gratitude instead of guilt.

DAY 60.

DIVERSITY MAKES OUR LIVES
MORE SOULFUL. WHEN WE
SEEK OUT DIFFERENT PEOPLE,
CULTURES, AND IDEAS, WE
ADD INCREDIBLE DEPTH TO
OUR HUMAN EXPERIENCE. WE
LEARN ABOUT OURSELVES AND
OUR WORLD IN WAYS THAT
MAKE US MORE THOUGHTFUL,
PASSIONATE, AND GENEROUS.

DAY 61.

"Laughter through tears is my favorite emotion."

—Truvy Jones, *Steel Magnolias*

There is nothing quite like the healing power of laughter. And we are so lucky that it often shows up when we need it most. Should it arrive on your doorstep, even in your darkest hour, let it in. Or perhaps I should say, let it out.

DAY 62.

Know the difference between regret and reflection. Regret keeps us stuck in the past and fills us with shame and frustration. Meaningful reflection helps us process our missteps, consequences, and lessons with acceptance and grace. It allows us to learn, live in the present moment, and move forward.

DAY 63.

Music quickly connects us to our hearts. We can hear the first few seconds of a song and be thrown into a beautiful memory, unearth and release a buried feeling, or simply become covered in joy. When we recognize the power of music, we understand that it is always there for us as a spiritual companion. As long as you have a favorite song, you are never alone.

DAY 64.

Freedom is fundamental to enjoying life. We must want it for ourselves and for others. We must create an atmosphere in our relationships where people feel free to wonder, ask questions, have their feelings, and be fully who they are without shame or judgment. There is a reason we are attracted to wildflowers, birds in flight, and ocean waves. They remind us that freedom is a natural, beautiful, and powerful part of being alive.

DAY 65.

Two pillars of sports psychology are positive self-talk and relaxation. Doubting ourselves makes winning much more difficult, if not impossible. Immense stress and tension block our ability to think clearly. Even if a team has lost nine games in a row, on the morning of the tenth game, each player must settle their mind and feel confident that a win is possible. These strategies can help us in all aspects of life: cultivate a calm mind and believe that whatever we want to achieve is possible.

DAY 66.

WHEN WE TEND TO THE NEEDS AND DESIRES OF THOSE WE LOVE, THEY FEEL SAFE. WHEN WE ALLOW THEM TO HELP US IN RETURN, WE BUILD TRUST THROUGH MUTUALITY. GIVING AND RECEIVING CREATES A SPIRITUAL CIRCLE OF CARE AROUND OUR RELATIONSHIPS.

DAY 67.

GOODNESS COMES FROM DOING WHAT FEELS GOOD.

Kindness feels good. Giving to others feels good. Doing the right thing (even when it isn't the easy thing) feels good. Honesty feels good. Fear and desperation make us think goodness is not an available option for solving our problems. Insecurity makes us think that we do not deserve to feel good. This causes us to make decisions and choose relationships that do not serve us. We deserve to do good and feel good. Know that goodness is possible.

DAY 68.

Leaders do more than direct others—they set the tone for our environments. When we choose leaders who lack moral character, their toxicity will always overshadow and hinder any possibility for progress. It is not enough to just go from one place to another; we need to get there in ways that are good and just. Real leaders lead with love. They know that is the only way to get anywhere worth going.

DAY 69.

It can be difficult to access gratitude during a tough time. When something awful happens to us, the idea that someone is asking us to look on the bright side can be hurtful and enraging. Gratitude is not a silver lining or the magical ability to turn a bad thing into a good thing. Gratitude is more of a cosmic life raft. It has the power to remove us from the center of our sinking ship so we can stay afloat as we process the pain and the damage. It does not ignore what is gone; it offers us refuge in what is still here.

DAY 70.

CALM YOUR MIND. NOURISH YOUR BODY. SOOTHE YOUR NERVOUS SYSTEM. FIND TOOLS AND FIND SUPPORT. SELF-CARE WILL NOT PREVENT THE TOUGH STUFF FROM HAPPENING BUT IT WILL PREVENT IT FROM TAKING YOU OUT. CARE HOLDS US TENDERLY WHEN LIFE'S TORNADOES COME SWEEPING THROUGH.

DAY 71.

Our relationships reflect the quality time we invest in them. As with anything in life, what we reap is what we sow. Time with friends cannot feel like an errand or a pit stop. When we carve out time for our loved ones, we must give them our undivided attention. Whether you spend the morning talking about nothing in particular, enjoying each other's company over coffee, or are diving deep into a discussion about something hard or important, they deserve our full presence. This is how we build trustworthy, long-lasting, intimate bonds.

DAY 72.

I love that *listen* and *silent* are spelled with the same letters. It is a reminder that to be fully aware as a listener, we must cultivate external and internal silence. When another person is speaking, it is unhelpful to crowd our minds with noise, thoughts, or possible responses. Only by being fully present and embracing true silence can we genuinely hear and feel the stories others share with us. Likewise, in the silence of solitude, we can listen clearly to ourselves.

DAY 73.

ALLOW THE WORDS "BECAUSE I RESPECT MYSELF" TO BE ENOUGH OF A REASON.

Sometimes we are asked to do things or be around people that do not make us feel safe or aligned with our values. It helps to remember that we respect ourselves by protecting ourselves. We are allowed to say no without fake excuses or elaborate explanations. Your time and energy are sacred. Set boundaries that acknowledge this.

DAY 74.

I once heard someone say that stress is manageable, but stress without recovery is not. If we have had a long day, week, or year, we need a recovery period. Our minds and bodies require rest and restoration so we can detox the stress and exhaustion that comes from everyday life. Pouring into ourselves is not indulgence; it is fuel. It is the fuel we need so we can keep going.

DAY 75.

People often compliment my mother on her vibrant energy. At almost seventy years old, she recently joined a local dance group that dresses in the theme of Dolly Parton and marches in Mardi Gras parades. She tries new recipes she finds on the Food Network or TikTok. She reads about interesting places, whether it is a restaurant in her neighborhood or a village in Portugal, and makes time to visit. Her way of life is a reminder that joy comes from trying new things and staying open to adventure.

DAY 76.

Without anger, how would we know something is wrong? Anger can be deeply motivating. It has fueled everything from righteous political movements to epic love songs. Owning our anger can bring deep healing and clarity to our perspective. We do not need to cut ourselves off from this powerful emotion. But we do need to regulate it, so it does not turn into violence. Violence is what happens when we believe that the only way to release anger is through harm.

DAY 77.

ONE WAY TO KEEP YOUR HEART TOGETHER WHEN THE STATE OF THE WORLD WEIGHS HEAVY ON IT IS TO SIMPLY HELP SOMEBODY. EVEN IF IT IS JUST ONE PERSON. ONE BREATH AT A TIME. ONE STEP AT A TIME. ONE PERSON AT A TIME.

DAY 78.

Closure gifts us calm after conflict. Sometimes we get closure through a healing exchange with others, and sometimes it is a solo journey. The other person involved is not always available to hold space for our feelings, take accountability for their actions, or make amends. We cannot give their behavior the power to control our tranquility. Your peace within never belongs in the hands of someone else. You can access closure through your own reflection and acceptance at any time.

DAY 79.

tough love

there is no such thing
as tough love
love is durable
never tough
its strength is lasting and powerful
but always tender
always
always
tender

DAY 80.

There is a motto in my hometown, New Orleans: *Laissez les bons temps rouler!* Let the good times roll! In a city that prioritizes joy, music, and dancing in the streets, this mantra encourages passing travelers to have fun. We don't have to wait for something "worth" celebrating. Today, we are alive. Find someone you love and rejoice in this day. Life will always be filled to the brim with difficulties. It is up to us to claim and center the good times whenever we can.

DAY 81.

The word *abracadabra* comes from the Hebrew phrase "ebrah k'dabri," meaning "I create as I speak." What we say to ourselves is what we create around us. When our inner dialogue is rooted in limitation, that becomes all we see. But when we speak to our potential—with wonder, positivity, and abundance—we begin to see a world full of possibility. Your magical thoughts have the power to become your magical life. The choice is yours. Just say the word.

DAY 82.

"I am my best work—a series of road maps, reports, recipes, doodles, and prayers from the front lines."

—Audre Lorde

Always remember that you are worthy. Always remember that you deserve to be seen and heard. And always, always remember that no one, not a single person in the entire universe, can be better at being you than *you*.

DAY 83.

Honor your sensitivities. To be deeply feeling is a superpower. It is not something to apologize for or wrap in shame. It means the world has not hardened your heart. It means your strength still has softness. It means you have not abandoned your connection to yourself in order to make everyone else more comfortable. Be proud of this.

DAY 84.

Forgive past versions of yourself. We have all said or done things we are not proud of. Feeling embarrassed is uncomfortable, but it is not entirely unhelpful. If we can avoid dwelling in shame, we can learn from our awkward or difficult periods and move on. Accepting and forgiving who we used to be helps us leave old versions of ourselves in the past so we can appreciate our growth and be proud of the person we are today.

DAY 85.

SPEND YOUR TIME WITH THE PEOPLE WHO MAKE EVEN GOING TO THE GROCERY STORE AN ADVENTURE.

Your time is your life. We are the sum of how we spend our time and who we spend it with. When we spend it with people who make us feel joyous and alive, we respect our sacred self and honor our one precious life.

DAY 86.

Allow yourself to be delighted by life's simple pleasures: watching the sun rise and set, savoring the first sip of your morning coffee, witnessing the world go by on a park bench, picking a flower, enjoying a friend's laugh, getting lost in a good book. These small easy moments feed our well-being and connect us to gratitude.

DAY 87.

"People think my life has been tough, but I think it has been a wonderful journey. The older you get, the more you realize it's not what happens, but how you deal with it."

—Tina Turner

Your narrative is yours to claim and reclaim. Let no one dictate your life story but you.

DAY 88.

We don't need to turn away from what makes us uncomfortable. We can meet these feelings, investigate their arrival, and accept their presence without sitting with them for too long. This is often more helpful than avoiding the feeling altogether. Avoidance does not make tough stuff disappear; it usually causes things to fester or manifest in a different, heavier form later. Instead, we can confront our emotions in a balanced, boundaried way—holding hello and goodbye with equal importance.

DAY 89.

WE MUST BE WILLING
TO CHANGE. REBELLING
AGAINST IT IS IMPRACTICAL
AND UNCOMFORTABLE.
IT FRACTURES OUR
RELATIONSHIPS, BLOCKS US
FROM OUR POTENTIAL, AND
LEAVES US FEELING STUCK.

DAY 90.

"You know what music is? God's little reminder that there's something else besides us in this universe. A harmonic connection between all living beings, everywhere, even the stars."

—Robin Williams

Music and the rest of the arts remind us we are never really alone. Our connection to this earth, this universe, is magical and miraculous.

DAY 91.

WHETHER OR NOT YOU CONSIDER YOURSELF RELIGIOUS, PRAYER IS A BEAUTIFUL GIFT AND PRACTICE. IN PRAYER, WE SURRENDER, SPEAK OUR TRUTH, AND WISH HEALING FOR OURSELVES AND OTHERS. IN PRAYER, WE SYNCHRONIZE WHAT IS MOST HUMAN ABOUT US AND WHAT IS MOST DIVINE.

DAY 92.

Perfectionism is sneaky; it creeps into how we work and parent, how we treat our bodies, and even how we create special moments for our loved ones. We can usually tell when it is present because it is accompanied by stress and tension. When we feel this, we must remember that we are imperfect by nature. People are beautiful and messy. Your life is a human journey and will never go completely as planned. That is okay. When we embrace this, feelings of freedom, flexibility, and joy flow within and around us.

DAY 93.

Maya Angelou often talked about never feeling alone when she entered intimidating rooms, because she brought with her the spirits of all who came before her. When we enter spaces that require courage, we, too, can envision ourselves accompanied by our friends who love us, our ancestors who came before us, and our heroes who have inspired us. Even when we think we are alone, the legacy of those who paved the way for us is always present, offering spiritual guidance and strength.

DAY 94.

Linger. When you enjoy something, stay in it for a while—a book, a bite, a sunny day, a walk with a friend, a community gathering. Do not rush joy. Do not hurry past new ideas or new people. As the Italians say, *La vita lenta*, the slow life. Maybe this pace is not available to us every moment of the day, but let's not be strangers to it.

DAY 95.

"That's what I consider true generosity: you give your all, and yet you always feel as if it costs you nothing."

—Simone de Beauvoir

Generosity is spiritual. It lives wholly in the moment with no expectation. This is what distinguishes it from transactional giving. There is no need attached to the deed.

DAY 96.

LIFE IS NOT ALWAYS SOMETHING WE CAN ORGANIZE, FIT INTO BOXES, OR EVENLY DISTRIBUTE BETWEEN COLUMNS ON A LIST. LIFE OFTEN BEHAVES MORE LIKE A MIGHTY OAK TREE WITH UNRULY ROOTS, BREAKING THE CONCRETE. WE DON'T TAME IT; WE FIND HARMONY WITH IT.

DAY 97.

In many cases, it is not that people *can't* read the room, but that they *won't*. They assume that what they want, think, and have to say is more important than everyone else. This self-centeredness often makes others feel alienated, uncomfortable, and hurt. Connection is not owed to anyone, we earn it together through care and community. Reading the room means respecting people's experiences and ideas as much as our own.

DAY 98.

Part of getting good sleep comes from valuing it and feeling worthy of it. When we don't feel deserving of rest or think of it as a waste of time, we experience anxiety the moment our head hits the pillow. When we respect that our mind, body, and spirit need time to release and recharge, we have reverence for sleep. We see it as a lifeline—one that is critical to our ability to process what goes on around us.

DAY 99.

Each of us is born loving ourselves. If you are ever around a baby, you will notice they already love themselves. They do not have shame. They do not think anything is wrong with the way they look or think. They delight in their silliness, drooling, giggling, chewing on their own toes. They are okay with who they are. As we get older, the world seems to chip away at this love. It tells us something is wrong with how we look, think, and feel. We start to believe that if we could just correct all the "wrong" stuff about us, then we would be allowed to love ourselves. Nope. You are always allowed to love yourself. The love you were born with belongs to you today.

DAY 100.

We must nourish our roots. What makes you feel grounded? Meditation? Visiting certain friends, elders, or places? Nature? Exercise? Alone time? Cooking? Baking? Helping others? We have no idea what the day can bring. To feel prepared, we need to know what makes us feel anchored. When our interior life is chaotic, everything we encounter will feel like one big exclamation point. But when we know how to access our spiritual center, we have the power to bring calm and okay-ness to whatever the day brings.

DAY 101.

"Almost everything will work again if you unplug it for a few minutes, including you."

—Anne Lamott

Take a break from the problem. Breathe, rest, stretch, and move. Struggling for long periods is neither sustainable nor productive. Walk away and come back to it.

DAY 102.

We outgrow relationships, jobs, and behaviors. As the author and main character of our life story, we always have the power to revise and remove what no longer belongs. It is helpful to reflect on whether any parts of our personal narrative are outdated and no longer true. Doing so clarifies our sense of self and honors our growth.

DAY 103.

Betrayal makes us feel lost, confused, and is often accompanied by drama and frenzy that only adds to our pain and overwhelm. Give yourself space to process what is yours to heal and what is for the other person to heal, knowing that recovery is possible, with or without the person who hurt you. We do not need to act from an open wound. Take time to emotionally stabilize, so that this one experience or person does not rob you of your ability to trust others.

DAY 104.

If you find yourself in a new circumstance or emotional state, pause, and adjust your care methods. When new needs arise, we must tend to them. Just as we drink extra water on a hot day, we might need more rest, support, or gentleness during stressful times. Significant changes require special attention. Allow your self-care practices to evolve to meet your current needs.

DAY 105.

THE EGO THINKS FIRST, THEN CREATES FEELINGS AROUND THOSE THOUGHTS; IT SENSES THREAT AND MANUFACTURES AN EMOTIONAL CASE. THE SPIRIT FEELS FIRST, THEN ADDS THOUGHTFULNESS; IT CREATES WISDOM BY BRINGING CAREFUL REFLECTION TO WHAT SHAKES YOUR HEART.

DAY 106.

"Sometimes good things fall apart so better things can fall together."

—Stevie Nicks

When relationships, jobs, or dreams fall apart, hold onto the idea that something more, bigger, or needed is coming in its place. I met my husband at a party for my ex-boyfriend. Our endings, even the ones that include heartbreak and disappointment, often lead to new beginnings.

DAY 107.

During conflict, it is helpful to pause for reflection before taking further action. It is also important to make sure we are pausing for perspective—not as a form of punishment. A useful pause is a break from the person or situation—it is not the silent treatment, or passive withdrawal. We can productively take space to assess our feelings, behavior, and expectations, as well as the other person's point of view. When we do this we can move forward in a way that shows care for everyone including ourselves.

DAY 108.

Find beauty. When the world around us feels extra gloomy, we can look for beauty in the same way Mr. Rogers encouraged us to "look for the helpers." Beauty reminds us of the brilliance of creation—a flower, a painting, a song, the smile of a child, a beautiful enduring relationship between friends or lovers. During moments of despair, we must remember that there are still good people (the helpers) and magical things (beauty) all around us. We just have to look for them.

DAY 109.

PROTECTION IS A DIVINE FORM OF SELF-LOVE. WE DESERVE TO PROTECT OURSELVES FROM PEOPLE AND PLACES THAT CAUSE US HARM. OUR INNER LIGHT DESERVES PROTECTION FROM MOTHS AND ENERGY VAMPIRES. IT IS ALWAYS OKAY TO DISTANCE YOURSELF FROM ENVIRONMENTS THAT DO NOT FEEL SAFE OR SUPPORTIVE.

DAY 110.

Whenever I visit my hometown, New Orleans, I marvel at the massive, ancient oak trees. Many of them are over seven hundred years old. I think about all they have seen—from violent wars to devastating hurricanes. And here they are, sturdy, beautiful, and present. They are not worried about the next storm.

DAY 111.

In judgment, we are so consumed by what we dislike about someone's behavior that we skip the step of wondering why or what in their life may be fueling it. We also tend to skip the step of wondering why the person or situation has triggered such a hefty emotional response in us. Wonder and curiosity lead us away from negativity and condemnation and toward empathy and understanding.

DAY 112.

"Now you better close your eyes, my child, for a moment . . . in order to be better in tune with the Infinite."

—The Wizard of Oz

We are magic; we are stardust. If we want to travel the galaxy, we can close our eyes, go within, and journey through our own personal universe. Self-connection is a fascinating, never-ending journey.

DAY 113.

IF YOU WANT TO FIND/BE YOUR AUTHENTIC SELF, YOU ARE GOING TO HAVE TO RESIST THE URGE TO ENTER ROOMS AND RELATIONSHIPS THAT REQUIRE YOU TO BE FAKE TO SURVIVE.

We deserve to spend our time in environments where we do not have to shrink, perform, or lie about our feelings and opinions. It may not be possible all the time, but when we fake it for too long, we dim our light, making it incredibly difficult to see ourselves clearly.

DAY 114.

"We need joy as we need air."

—Maya Angelou

Joy is not an extravagance. It is not something we are only allowed to have when things are going well. Even when everything is a mess, we still need joy. It is the energizing life force that helps us endure darkness. With it, we find grace, humor, and beauty in life's complications and contradictions. Joy lightens the weight of our burdens and grief, even if only for a moment. Regardless of what you are going through, leave the door open for joy. It is what makes the unbearable bearable.

DAY 115.

on "doing the work"

do the inner work
not
only to keep your own soul tidy
but to be able to clean up
our world
it is a mess in need of angels
be one if you can
that is the point of all of this
I am sure of it

DAY 116.

Calming down is always an option. This seems so simple, but when we are in the heat of the moment—running late, panicked, upset, or overwhelmed—we forget that we can relax our inflamed mind before we try to do anything else. The next time you feel your anxiety heighten, pause, have a glass of water, take a few breaths, or reach out for support. Connect to calm.

DAY 117.

The more we do something, the better we get at it. We become better at sharing our feelings the more we let them flow. We go deeper into pessimism the more we give into it. We become powerful listeners by listening. Incredible lovers by loving. Kindness is a habit. Self-kindness is a habit. Likewise, complaining, negativity, and unkindness are habits. We are the habits we choose, and it is never too late to choose ones that serve our highest self.

DAY 118.

WE ARE GIVEN A CHANCE TO
START OVER EVERY DAY. WE
GET TO BEGIN AGAIN AND AGAIN
AND AGAIN. IT IS ONE OF LIFE'S
GREAT MIRACULOUS GIFTS.
TAKE ADVANTAGE OF THIS. GIVE
YOURSELF A FRESH START
IF THAT IS WHAT YOU NEED.
LEAVE THE PAST IN THE PAST.
THE SUN CAME UP TODAY
FOR YOU; LET ITS LIGHT IN.

DAY 119.

Your social circle is not always your healing circle. When we are going through a specific painful experience, it is critical that we allow ourselves to find comfort with those who can offer support and relate to what we are going through. This healing circle may not include the people we are used to relying on, and that is okay. We must not try to fit an emotional square peg into a round hole. Not everyone in our life belongs everywhere in our life or in every season of it.

DAY 120.

Human beings have built-in bravery. It does not come from an outside source; it flows from the center of our aliveness. As Brene Brown reminds us, the root of the word *courage* is *cor*—the Latin word for heart. To know its location is to know where to find it when you are in need. Put your hands over your heart, close your eyes, and say, "The courage I need is right here."

DAY 121.

HOPE FOLLOWS LOVE. WHEN WE LOVE PEOPLE, WE WILL ALWAYS HAVE HOPE FOR HUMANITY. WHEN WE LOVE OUR COUNTRY, WE WILL ALWAYS HAVE HOPE FOR UNITY. WHEN WE LOVE OUR WORLD, WE WILL ALWAYS HAVE HOPE FOR ITS HEALING.

DAY 122.

We greatly benefit from macro pauses—a good night's sleep, an extended period alone with our thoughts, a vacation, or time away from our work and chores. We can also make time for micro pauses—a moment to appreciate the shape of the clouds, notice a bird or a flower, or focus on our breath. These mini moments are incredible gifts to our nervous system, removing us from the stress of go-go-go, so we may be embraced by calm, if only for a minute.

DAY 123.

Self-forgiveness is the acknowledgment that you are human and deserving of mercy, tenderness, and grace. We are often hardest on ourselves. We create impossible standards and punish ourselves when we fall short. It does not have to be this way. You are allowed to forgive yourself. We are allowed to forgive ourselves. We all cause harm, whether we mean to or not. But when we reflect on our actions, take accountability, offer an apology, and create space for repair, the final step in this journey is forgiveness. For ourselves and everyone else.

DAY 124.

SOME PEOPLE ARE GOOD AT
LOVING US, AND SOME PEOPLE
ARE REALLY BAD AT IT.
DON'T JUDGE YOURSELF FOR
PICKING SOMEONE WHO COULD
NOT RISE TO THE OCCASION.
KNOW THAT FINDING LOVE
IS A GREAT EXPERIMENT,
ONE THAT OVERFLOWS
WITH LESSONS FROM BOTH
JOY AND HEARTACHE.

DAY 125.

in your own hands

discipline
is no nagging mother
or disappointed father
it is a friendly voice
it is your voice
reminding you
that everything you want is yours
if you start today

DAY 126.

The relationships we have are based on what we *believe* we deserve from others. The work we pursue is based on what we *believe* our potential to be. Our habits reflect what we *believe* is good enough for us, and the ways we cope are based on what we *believe* is the only way we will feel better. Recognizing this helps us understand clearly why it is essential to seek the tools and support needed for healthy self-esteem, a calm mind, and a full heart. It is from this foundation that everything we believe about ourselves and the world is formed.

DAY 127.

TRANSACTIONAL RELATIONSHIPS WILL GET YOU SOMEWHERE. THAT IS FOR SURE. BUT SOULFUL RELATIONSHIPS WILL ALWAYS BRING YOU HOME TO YOURSELF. THEY WILL REMIND YOU THAT, AS TONI MORRISON SAID, "YOU ARE YOUR BEST THING." IT IS THE DIFFERENCE BETWEEN A HANDSHAKE AND A HUG.

DAY 128.

It is infinitely more enjoyable to wade into warm, salty waters than it is to submerge ourselves into the harsh cold. Similarly, if we are having a hard day or moving through a painful period, we must try not to put ourselves in situations that will only add a layer of discomfort to our current state. Why pile on? Give yourself permission to cancel plans, put off nonurgent appointments, do less, and go to bed early. Find your warm waters.

DAY 129.

HOPE BEGINS IN OUR IMAGINATION, AS DOES DESPAIR. WE HAVE THE POWER TO PAINT A PICTURE OF POSSIBILITY OR OF ABSOLUTE DISASTER. WE MUST BE MINDFUL OF THE THOUGHTS WE NURTURE. OUR CREATIVE THINKING CAN AND WILL COLOR THE WORLD AROUND US.

DAY 130.

Everyone deserves a fair chance to have a good life. We must want that for everyone. The desire for justice and equality comes from a peaceful, loving heart. From a heart that does not believe any human being is superior to another. From a heart that believes we all deserve to be okay, to be safe, to be loved, and to have access to opportunities. Every heart has the potential to hold this much love for humanity.

DAY 131.

WE MUST SPEND OUR LIVES CREATING, NURTURING, AND CELEBRATING LOVE. THERE IS NO BETTER USE OF OUR TIME. EACH MORNING, ASK YOURSELF: HOW BIG CAN MY HEART GET TODAY? HOW MANY PEOPLE CAN I FIT IN IT? HOW FAR CAN I STRETCH MY LOVE? LOVE IS OUR ONLY REAL LEGACY.

DAY 132.

"All you need is faith, trust, and a little bit of pixie dust."

—J. M. Barrie

Faith, as Martin Luther King Jr. said, is taking the next step even when you can't see the whole staircase. To have faith, we need trust. And it also helps to have something more—pixie dust, a belief in magic, a higher power, the universe, or the energy of our ancestors. There is amazing comfort in knowing a greater energy walks with us into the unknown.

DAY 133.

JEALOUSY DOESN'T HAVE TO BE TOXIC. IT CAN ACTUALLY BE USEFUL. INSTEAD OF LETTING ENVY TURN INTO NEGATIVITY, WE CAN TREAT IT AS INFORMATION—A SIGNAL GUIDING US TOWARD OUR DESIRES AND GOALS.

DAY 134.

A friend recently told me her top three needs in a romantic relationship are freedom, integrity, and pleasure. We don't often put pleasure on the list of our desires, but what is the quality of our lives without it? Our relationships cannot just be labor. They must be fun. They must be enjoyable. Good love and a good life include pleasure.

DAY 135.

We can't change people or force them into accountability. We can't fix difficult people, make them happier, more responsible, or less selfish. The best we can do is accept them for who they are and where they are, then decide what type of relationship we are willing to have with them, if any. People are not perfect, and neither are relationships, but we are allowed to have standards and expectations, so we do not constantly find ourselves disappointed.

DAY 136.

When we set goals, we often focus on what we want to *have* rather than how we want to *feel*. This can leave us feeling alone or empty at our finish lines. When our goals reach beyond the material and connect to our emotional, relational, and spiritual life, we are much more likely to feel a sense of purpose and holistic happiness.

DAY 137.

"There is always something to do. There are hungry people to feed, naked people to clothe, sick people to comfort and make well. And while I don't expect you to save the world I do think it's not asking too much for you to love those with whom you sleep, share the happiness of those whom you call friend, engage those among you who are visionary, and remove from your life those who offer you depression, despair, and disrespect."

—Nikki Giovanni

DAY 138.

"I have a huge and savage conscience that won't let me get away with things."

—Octavia Butler

It can be all too easy to take amoral shortcuts. To have a conscience is to hear your heartbeat in your mind. Let it guide you and keep what is sacred within you safe. Let it be the leading voice in your decision-making process. Let it be loud. And giant. And always win.

DAY 139.

SOULMATES. LOTS AND LOTS OF SOULMATES.

Soulmates are not reserved for romantic love. Friends make for powerful soulmates too. Feeling divinely understood is so important. Allow for soul connections to flourish in abundant and unexpected ways. Maybe you find "the one" in this life or maybe you find "the some."

DAY 140.

Spirituality without practice is ego. When we talk the talk, we must walk the walk. We read spiritual texts, self-help books, and inspirational quotes, we study religions, but how often are we practicing our principles? Lessons learned are only valuable when we put them into action. Our spiritual values belong in the real world, shifting our behavior and pushing us toward our highest selves.

DAY 141.

QUITTING IS NOT ALWAYS GIVING UP. SOMETIMES IT IS THE ONLY WAY TO CREATE SPACE FOR A NEW DREAM. WHEN WE CHANGE OR THE WORLD AROUND US CHANGES, WE CAN LET OUR GOALS, MINDS, AND HEARTS CHANGE TOO. QUITTING IS A FORM OF LETTING GO. LETTING GO IS A PART OF BEING ALIVE.

DAY 142.

We do not have to like our past, but if we have even an ounce of gratitude for where we are today, we can respect it. Every wrong turn, every misguided decision and naive idea, led you to where you are now. When we respect where we have been and what we have gone through, we see every step and misstep as a necessary part of our journey. This helps us move forward with ease, courage, and humility.

DAY 143.

CONFIDENCE BELONGS TO THOSE WHO CREATE AND NURTURE IT. IT IS A PRACTICE, NOT A GIFT. IT IS NOT SOMETHING PEOPLE ARE BORN WITH AND OTHERS ARE NOT. CONFIDENCE FLOWS FROM POSITIVE AND ENCOURAGING SELF-TALK, AND IS FURTHERED BY HONEST, HELPFUL COMMUNITY.

DAY 144.

Everyone needs and deserves attention, but we must be mindful of how we request it. Resorting to negative behaviors like lashing out, passive-aggressive signaling, and moodiness can push others away and leave us feeling isolated. Maturity involves learning to regulate your emotional self before requesting attention. When we are open, direct, clear, and kind, we foster healthier, more secure relationships. We invite genuine connection and avoid the loneliness that comes from indirect or unhealthy attempts to gain attention.

DAY 145.

IF SELF-LOVE SAYS,

"I LOVE YOU,"

SELF-CARE SAYS, "PROVE IT."

* SELF-CARE IS THE PRACTICE
CREATED BY YOU, FOR YOU,
THAT PROVES HOW MUCH
YOU LOVE YOURSELF.

DAY 146.

TAKE A BREAK FROM PLANNING AND PLEASING. ALLOW YOURSELF SPACE TO SIMPLY BE AND DREAM. WE ALL HAVE THE POWER TO BE VISIONARIES, AT LEAST FOR OUR OWN PATH. UNSTRUCTURED TIME TO ALIGN OUR THOUGHTS, FEELINGS, AND INTUITION ALLOWS SPACE FOR RENEWAL AND SPIRITUAL PROGRESS.

DAY 147.

"What are you going to do? Everything, is my guess. It will be a little messy, but embrace the mess. It will be complicated, but rejoice in the complications. It will not be anything like what you think it will be like, but surprises are good for you. And don't be frightened: you can always change your mind. I know: I've had four careers and three husbands."

—Nora Ephron

DAY 148.

Does the sea ever say, "I am not the ocean"? Would the river ever discriminate against a single raindrop? Does the pond ever consider the lake to be anything less than kin? And do you think the stream would ever dream of feeling inferior to the channel, or the channel ever regard the stream in any other way than magnificent in her soothing beauty?

The natural world flows as one with great respect for its many manifestations. We, too, must live this way with one another.

DAY 149.

THE OPPOSITE OF SELF-CARE IS SELF-ABANDONMENT. YOU ARE A PERSON, JUST LIKE EVERYONE ELSE, AND DESERVE TO BE SEEN, HELD, AND CONSIDERED. THROUGH CARE WE CAN COME HOME TO OURSELVES AND HONOR OUR WORTH.

DAY 150.

It is okay to feel sad. We fall in love with the songs we can dance to and the songs we can cry to. Sadness is a tender emotion that connects us deeply to love, compassion, and empathy. We sometimes hide our sadness or cover it in shame, believing it is a weakness or that it will make others uncomfortable. In reality, we all benefit from the full spectrum of our emotional offerings—from the upbeat to the melancholy. Honesty, intimacy, and vulnerability connect us to ourselves and others.

DAY 151.

REAL FRIENDS CHEER US ON AND CHALLENGE US TO MEET OUR POTENTIAL. THEY SUPPORT OUR MORAL COMPASS, OUR PERSONAL GROWTH, OUR HOPES FOR OUR LIVES, AND OUR DUTY TO THE WORLD AROUND US. THEY ARE FRIENDS WITH WHO WE ARE TODAY AND WHO WE WANT TO BE IN THE FUTURE.

DAY 152.

Never underestimate the power of art. It can soothe us after a long day, provoke new ideas when we feel stagnant, create needed emotional release, and help us understand our own feelings and experiences better. We think we don't need art until our hearts break and there is only one song or poem that helps us put it back together. Or when we have had a stressful day and finally get to relax on the couch with our favorite film. Art reminds us of our connection to each other and our power to inspire one another.

DAY 153.

OUR TEARS CARRY FEELINGS, INFORMATION, AND MEMORIES. A GOOD CRY IS A RELEASE AND AN OPPORTUNITY TO START FRESH. WATER HAS CLEANSING PROPERTIES. THAT IS WHY IT FEELS SO GOOD TO JUMP IN THE OCEAN, SIT IN THE TUB, OR TAKE A LONG SHOWER. WATER WASHES LAYERS OF OUR BURDENS AWAY.

DAY 154.

EMPIRES FALL. POLITICAL REGIMES SHIFT AND CHANGE. MACHINES BREAK AND ARE REPLACED WITH NEW MODELS. OUR STUFF GOES OUT OF STYLE. BIG BUSINESSES BOOM AND FADE. AND THEN THERE'S LOVE, IN ALL ITS QUIET CONFIDENCE, STILL HERE, STILL THE HEART OF EVERYTHING, STILL THE POINT OF IT ALL.

DAY 155.

Love is an energetic feeling *and* a collection of principles. It is comprised of kindness, respect, integrity, safety, compassion, and commitment. When we believe in universal love for all of humanity, we understand that our beliefs about love walk beside us everywhere we go. Love belongs in our politics, our friend and family life, our work life, and our community spaces.

DAY 156.

Can today be a blessing? Can we be a blessing to someone in need? Appreciating goodness and doing good for others will always make you feel better. We do not have control of much in this world, but we have control over how and where we shine our own light. We have control over how we treat others. We have control over how we view the world. We have control over whether we focus on counting our blessings or our worries.

DAY 157.

WHEN WE PRACTICE
FORGETTING—EVERYTHING
WE TRY TO FORGET
BECOMES A GHOST LURKING
IN OUR SHADOWS.

WHEN WE PRACTICE
FORGIVING—EVERYTHING
WE FORGIVE BECOMES
AN ANGEL, A GUIDE THAT
LIVES IN OUR LIGHT.

DAY 158.

Speaking out ends the pain of silence. Silence can seem like a good place to hide, but it keeps us in the dark. We cannot spend our lives in an uneasy place where we cannot see ourselves or anyone else clearly. We deserve to live in the light, in the warm presence of our truth and our dignity.

DAY 159.

THERE IS NO ONE WAY TO CALM YOUR MIND AND CONNECT TO PRESENCE. WE CAN SIT IN STILLNESS, REPEAT A MANTRA, DO YOGA, MAKE TEA, KNIT, TAKE A LONG WALK, OR EVEN WASH THE DISHES. MEDITATION WORKS BEST WHEN IT WORKS FOR YOU.

DAY 160.

SCARCITY BLOCKS OUR ABILITY TO BE HAPPY FOR AND LIVE IN HARMONY WITH OTHERS. WHEN WE LIVE WITH ABUNDANCE, WE FEEL NO NEED TO GRASP WITH GREED, WE VALUE SHARING AND DO IT FREELY, FREQUENTLY, AND WITH AN OPEN HEART. WE ARE RELAXED AND TRUSTING.

DAY 161.

"What they call you is one thing. What you answer to is something else."

—Lucille Clifton

You are always in possession of your dignity. No one has the power to rob you of your personhood or your sacred self. Let no one define you but you.

DAY 162.

inevitabilities

it will get messy (your life)
it will break (your heart)
but
oh, the joy
of all you learn
and the power you gain
when you figure out
how to clean it up
and make your
heart whole
again
& again
& again & again

DAY 163.

OUR LIVES BECOME AN EXTRAORDINARY QUILT WITH BEAUTY IN ALL THE PATCHES, DIFFERENT COLORS, MATERIALS, TECHNIQUES, AND CONTRIBUTORS. IT IS SOMETHING WE MAKE, AND IT ALSO MAKES US.

DAY 164.

You never know. You never know how much and in what directions you will change. You never know what about you will be true today and irrelevant tomorrow. You never know when joy or despair will visit, or who will be there holding your hand through either or both. I think we could all benefit from leaving a little room to be surprised and delighted by the unknown.

DAY 165.

Collaborators, co-dreamers, and co-conspirators supercharge our ideas, dreams, and visions for the world. They can help us stay focused when we feel exhausted and inspire us to reach even further than we thought possible. You don't have to go it alone. Allow others to amplify your light.

DAY 166.

ACCEPTANCE WRAPS EVERY VERSION OF YOU AND YOUR EVOLVING LIFE IN GRATITUDE. IT LETS RELATIONSHIPS RUN THEIR COURSE WITHOUT FEAR AND GUILT. IT LOVES YOUR BODY THROUGH CHANGE WITHOUT SHAME AND SORROW. AND IT WELCOMES NEW SEASONS WITHOUT DISAPPOINTMENT AND DEFIANCE.

DAY 167.

When we replace wanting to win with wanting to learn, we don't fear failure or rejection, we see it simply as a part of life. Learners, especially those with spiritual curiosity, challenge their minds and allow their experiences to inform their hearts and shape their souls. When we live with this energy, we gain wisdom from our path and have more fun in the exploration.

DAY 168.

THERE IS WISDOM IN THE WAVES OF THE OCEAN. EVERYTHING IN LIFE COMES AND GOES, AND COMES AND GOES, AND COMES AND GOES, AGAIN, AND AGAIN, AND AGAIN . . . LIFE'S TIDES ARE NOT OURS TO CONTROL. WE MUST LEARN TO FLOAT IN THEM INSTEAD OF FIGHT AGAINST THEM.

DAY 169.

"We have to continually be jumping off cliffs and developing our wings on the way down."

—Kurt Vonnegut

Know when to stretch. Sometimes we can only learn how to do something by . . . doing it. We have to figure it out in real life, in front of watchful eyes, in the face of consequences, applause, or indifference. We are messy. We are clumsy. And we are something else too—we are brave. We are divine. We are alive.

DAY 170.

AN UNHEALTHY COMPETITIVE SPIRIT MAKES INTIMACY WITH OTHERS IMPOSSIBLE. WE CANNOT FORM A TRUSTING BOND WITH ANYONE WHO IS CONSTANTLY COMPARING THEMSELVES TO US. LOVING RELATIONSHIPS MUST SUPPORT AND CELEBRATE OUR WORTH, NOT APPRAISE IT.

DAY 171.

Our thoughts and emotions are in constant conversation, and sometimes even conflict, within us. This can blur the line between what is real and what is true, what is a feeling and what is a fact. When we put our thoughts on paper, we unload and better understand them. Writing or journaling helps us release what's stuck, track our growth, and see our lives more clearly.

DAY 172.

Fire reminds us it only takes a spark to create a flame. And with that flame we can light the way for ourselves and generations to come. We cannot pass the torch to others until we create and harness our own light within. No one is naturally more vibrant than another. There are simply those who tend to their light and those who do not.

DAY 173.

SOLITUDE GIFTS US A SLOW DANCE WITH OUR OWN THOUGHTS. IN SILENCE WE HEAR OURSELVES CLEARLY. OUR IMAGINATION HAS ROOM TO RUN, OUR BODIES CAN RELAX, OUR MINDS CAN CONNECT WITH OUR HEARTS, AND WE CAN ENJOY . . . OURSELVES.

DAY 174.

"Love is an action, never simply a feeling."

—bell hooks

When we love someone, we must be all in. We must be wholly committed to expressing our love through our words and actions. And if someone tells us they love us, it is healthy to expect this from them. Good love is reliable, thoughtful, kind, moving, and growing. It is not passive.

DAY 175.

DON'T UNDERESTIMATE THE SIMPLE STUFF: A FEW MINUTES OF SUNSHINE, A DEEP BREATH, A GLASS OF WATER, A BREAK, A REST, A MOMENT TO YOURSELF. THESE LITTLE MOMENTS OF RESTORATION HAVE THE POWER TO TURN YOUR ENTIRE DAY AROUND.

DAY 176.

"Hope has two beautiful daughters; their names are Anger and Courage. Anger at the way things are, and Courage to see that they do not remain as they are."

—St. Augustine

It helps to remember that there is a place for anger in hope. Hope is not delusion; it does not deny what's wrong; it is hell-bent on righting it.

DAY 177.

There is wisdom on the other side of our struggles and sometimes victory feels sweeter because we have overcome a difficult battle. That said, every worthwhile experience doesn't have to be hard. We can also grow, learn, and become with ease. A soft, gentle approach to work, love, and life is allowed.

DAY 178.

YOUR LIFE'S GREATEST DISCOVERY MAY JUST BE THAT YOU ARE YOUR OTHER HALF, YOUR KNIGHT IN SHINING ARMOR, AND THE ONE YOU HAVE BEEN WAITING FOR YOUR WHOLE LIFE.

A friend of mine once told me, "Find your happiest single self, then be that in a relationship." Whether they be platonic, familial, or romantic, all of our relationships benefit from us feeling whole.

DAY 179.

AUTHENTICITY IS HONESTY
IN ACTION. TO BE AUTHENTIC
IS TO ACKNOWLEDGE AND
EXPRESS YOUR TRUE FEELINGS
AND THOUGHTS. WE BLOCK
THE FLOW OF AUTHENTICITY
WHEN WE TRY TO BE PERFECT
OR AGREEABLE INSTEAD OF
REAL, SINCERE, AND HUMAN.

DAY 180.

"If your compassion does not include yourself, it is incomplete."

—Jack Kornfield

We can be our own harshest critic. That is why we must offer ourselves compassion. Without self-compassion—genuine care and concern for our own hardships—we disconnect from our ability to heal and move forward with love and openness.

DAY 181.

SHAME DOESN'T TELL THE TRUTH. IT AMPLIFIES THE VOLUME OF OUR WORST THOUGHTS. WHEN WE KNOW HOW SHAME WORKS, WE CAN CALL IT OUT WHEN IT COMES UP, AND ADVOCATE WITHIN FOR MORE HELPFUL, HONEST THINKING.

DAY 182.

KNOW WHICH EXPERIENCES ARE WORTH HOLDING ON TO AND WHICH ARE WORTH LETTING GO OF. IF YOU WANT A FRESH SLATE TOMORROW, CLEAN IT OFF TODAY.

DAY 183.

Give thanks to the aliveness your body has offered you today. If you are reading this right now, your body has gifted you this moment in time. *Thank you, body.* Your relationship with your body is like any other relationship—it needs love, kindness, and care.

DAY 184.

Our weirdness is our superpower. It is the manifestation of our unique way of thinking and seeing the world. What makes us different or "weird" is what makes our perspective interesting and important. It is the thing we have that no one else does. So be weird. Hang with other weird people. Do weird stuff together. Our world benefits from our weirdness.

DAY 185.

BEGIN TODAY KNOWING
YOU ARE LOVABLE.

LOOK IN THE MIRROR AND SAY,

"I AM LOVABLE. I AM WORTHY
OF LOVE, JUST AS I AM."

* WE BUILD BEAUTIFUL RELATIONSHIPS
AND A BEAUTIFUL LIFE WHEN
THIS IS OUR FOUNDATION.

DAY 186.

NOT EVERYTHING CAN BE A BIG DEAL OR TAKEN PERSONALLY. WE HAVE BAD DAYS, LOSE OUR WALLETS, MISS THE TRAIN. WORK, FRIENDS, AND STRANGERS ANNOY US. THIS IS NOT NOTHING, BUT IT CAN'T BE EVERYTHING. INCONVENIENCE IS NOT CATASTROPHE.

DAY 187.

"We could say that the word *mindfulness* is pointing to being one with our experiences, not dissociating, being right there when our hand touches the doorknob or the telephone rings or feelings of all kinds arise. The word *mindfulness* describes being right where we are."

—Pema Chödrön

Mindfulness belongs to all of us at all times. We don't need to be an expert; we just need to be present.

DAY 188.

Moments of pure freedom are critical to personal joy—standing in the rain, staying up late dancing, walking barefoot in the park, dressing up for no reason. These small but meaningful rebellions add flavor and spice to our lives, reminding us how good it feels to leave the rules and other people's opinions behind.

DAY 189.

<u>5 things you can do if you are feeling lost:</u>

1. Find stillness (pausing is not quitting).

2. Breathe.

3. Think (consider the next step rather than the greater destination).

4. Ask for help.

5. Make a map (study others who found themselves after periods of lostness).

DAY 190.

Our need to be nurtured never ends. One of the great gifts of adulthood is the power to reparent our inner child. To hear their needs and feelings and offer the support they never had. To offer them safety and soothe their wounds. Healing happens our whole lives. We are not stuck with our past wounds. We can tend to them today.

DAY 191.

UNFORGIVENESS IS LIFE WITH A STORM BENEATH OUR SKIN. WHEN WE REACH FOR FORGIVENESS, ESPECIALLY SELF-FORGIVENESS, WE CLEAR THE CLOUDS. THE ANGER, DISAPPOINTMENT, AND RESENTMENT DISSIPATE . . . WE BEGIN TO FEEL THE WARMTH OF THE SUN AGAIN.

DAY 192.

Our jobs may give us a sense of purpose, or they may simply serve a practical function. Toni Morrison said, "You are not the work you do; you are the person you are." When we fill our lives with variety, community, and meaningful relationships, we feel less pressure to center our identity on any one thing. This frees us from the limiting idea that our job is the most important thing about us.

DAY 193.

DON'T SPEND TOO MUCH TIME TRYING TO CONVINCE OTHERS TO LOOK AT YOU THE WAY YOU WANT THEM TO OR THE WAY YOU SEE YOURSELF. INSTEAD, MOVE THROUGH THE WORLD WITH LOVE, HONESTY, AND INTEGRITY, TRUSTING THAT ALL YOUR CONNECTIONS (AND DISCONNECTIONS) ARE MEANT TO BE.

DAY 194.

LIVE YOUR LIFE. TAKE RISKS. BE WILD AND FREE AND COLORFUL. DANCE IN PUBLIC. FALL IN LOVE. MAKE NEW FRIENDS. BEFRIEND YOURSELF. SHARE. BELLY LAUGH. CRY. AND FOR GOODNESS' SAKE, BE KIND! WE NEED KINDNESS MOST OF ALL.

DAY 195.

right now

would you like to experience the moment
or control it?
it is not possible to do both, beloved.

DAY 196.

“‘Thank You’ is the best prayer that anyone could say. I say that one a lot. Thank you expresses extreme gratitude, humility, understanding.”

—Alice Walker

When you want to access gratitude, simply start with *thank you*. Acknowledge everything around you that makes it possible for you to be here, now.

DAY 197.

"The best things in life aren't things."

—Art Buchwald

Praise and material things can create a sense of pride and momentary satisfaction, but they rarely yield a truly content heart. The road to real success is more often paved with simple joys, loving relationships, generosity, and gratitude. This way of life is grounding, purposeful, and emotionally enriching.

DAY 198.

Very few actions yield neutral results. We are usually building up or chipping away at ourselves, our bonds, and our world. When we ignore the voice within, whispering our needs, it eventually yells out in discomfort or pain. When we neglect our friends and family, it eventually alienates us from those we love. When we treat our world with indifference, we only add to its problems. On the flip side, when we listen to ourselves, pour into our loved ones, and care for our world, we learn the sacred power of positive participation.

DAY 199.

HONESTY FEELS BETTER THAN PERFECTION, POPULARITY, AND ADMIRATION. WHEN WE WALK IN OUR TRUTH, WE LOSE THE DESIRE TO COMPROMISE OURSELVES IN ORDER TO BE LIKED. WE HAVE PEACE, EASE, AND CONFIDENCE IN BEING OURSELVES. WHO WE ARE IS ENOUGH.

DAY 200.

YOU RESPECT YOUR LIFE BY KNOWING IT MATTERS. YOU RESPECT YOUR NEIGHBOR BY KNOWING THEY MATTER. YOU RESPECT YOUR COMMUNITY BY KNOWING IT MATTERS. PEACE AND FAIRNESS FLOW FROM DIGNITY.

DAY 201.

" I really don't think life is about the I-could-have-beens. Life is only about the I-tried-to-do. I don't mind the failure but I can't imagine that I'd forgive myself if I didn't try."

—Nikki Giovanni

Every adventure, big and small, begins with trying.

DAY 202.

YOU ARE ALLOWED TO DO LESS. WE DON'T HAVE TO CHECK EVERYTHING OFF THE LIST TODAY. SOMETIMES, THE GREATEST GIFT WE GIVE OURSELVES IS THE REMINDER THAT THERE IS ALWAYS TOMORROW. IT DOESN'T ALL HAVE TO GET DONE RIGHT NOW. GIVE YOURSELF A BREAK.

DAY 203.

"To let go does not mean to get rid of. To let go means to let be. When we let be with compassion, things come and go on their own."

—Jack Kornfield

Exhale. Let be.

DAY 204.

at every age

visit with elders
let their memories dance with your worldview
let their sacred knowledge pleasantly spin you
and your opinions
round and round and round
visit with children
let their "why nots" and "how comes"
cover your certainties
keep doing this 'til you learn something
it takes a village to become wise

DAY 205.

NOTHING CAN GROW WITHOUT SPACE TO GROW.

Space can take many forms; it might look like time, distance, or planting ourselves in a specific place. Just like roots need room to grow deep and strong, we, too, need space to expand into our fullest self.

DAY 206.

MORAL CLARITY PROTECTS THE SOUL. WHEN YOU KNOW WHAT IS RIGHT AND WHAT IS WRONG, YOUR HUMANITY SITS FIRMLY AT THE CENTER OF YOUR DECISIONS AND YOUR LIFE.

DAY 207.

Whether we are in search of partnership or friendship, we must seek similar values, energy, interests, expectations, and availability or we will be left feeling insecure, overlooked, and out of sync. A love worthy of your time is built on shared devotion, where attachment feels safe, and no one is left with less than they give. We must be open to finding it and be prepared to exit relationships that don't have it.

DAY 208.

THERE IS NO SUCH THING AS A HELL MAYBE.

Let your "yeses" be a *hell yes*! And your "nos" be a *hell no*! "Maybe" is a foggy, gray area. When we choose it too often or linger in too long, it creates dull, stagnant energy. We deserve color and vibrancy. We deserve to spend our time in ways that feel intentional, purposeful, alive, and fun.

DAY 209.

When in search of belonging—whether it is a job, school, relationship, or social group—remember, connection must feel good and right to you, too. It isn't just about making the cut, being chosen, or getting the invitation. There is not a room in the world, no matter how competitive or exclusive, that is worthy of your time and life if it doesn't light you up.

DAY 210.

"I don't divide the world into the weak and the strong, or the successes and the failures . . . *I divide the world into the learners and nonlearners.*"

—Benjamin Barber

We are never done learning. When we encounter those who refuse change or hold rigid, unyielding views, they are usually the same people who feel they know or have seen enough. A learner's mindset keeps life an ever-unfolding adventure.

DAY 211.

MANTRA FOR STEADINESS:

YOU ARE PEACEFUL, YOU ARE CALM, YOU ARE HEALTHY, YOU ARE HAPPY, YOU ARE SAFE, YOU ARE JOYFUL, YOU ARE LOVED, LOVED, LOVED.

DAY 212.

Not everything needs our opinion. You are allowed to say, *I don't know*. You are allowed to say, *I need more time to think about how I feel*. You are allowed to say, *I don't know enough about it yet to give an informed opinion*. You are allowed to say, *I would need to learn more, before I say more*. We do not need to feel pressured to respond to everything that goes on the minute it occurs. The world may be moving more quickly than ever, but we still need the space to feel, contemplate, synthesize, and sit in our questions with trusted friends and resources.

DAY 213.

“Memories are simply moments

that refuse to be ordinary.”

—Diane Keaton

May we always indulge in memories. May we honor them each time they visit. May we close our eyes and let them take us back to those extraordinary moments, the ones that made us so damn grateful to be alive.

DAY 214.

LIFE CAN CHANGE YOU. OR YOU CAN CHANGE WITH LIFE. WE ARE IN MOTION. EVERYTHING WE KNOW IS ALWAYS MOVING. WITH TENSION, WITH JOY, AND EVERYTHING IN BETWEEN. WE CAN WRESTLE WITH THIS ENERGY, OR WE CAN DANCE WITH IT. THE CHOICE IS COMPLETELY UP TO US.

DAY 215.

"My friend Maud once said, 'There are times when we must speak, not because you are going to change the other person, but because if you don't speak, they have changed you.'"

—Melissa McEwan

Silence doesn't change the world. It changes us. It shrinks us. We deserve to take up space and be heard. Our communities are safer and healthier when we use our voices and share our stories, especially in the face of tyranny and injustice. Turn up the volume. Let love be loud.

DAY 216.

“Value making a difference more than making a fortune.”

—Lynne Twist

The real joys of life come from the relationships we cultivate, the contributions we make to our communities, and from being proud of how we spend our time and energy. When we allow money to be too central, we lose perspective on what is really important and risk falling down the slippery slope of corruption and not enoughness.

DAY 217.

how to do the thing you are afraid to do

grab fear's hand
grab hope's hand
start walking

DAY 218.

Laughter is a restorative break from our worries and problems. It feels good to laugh. It feels even better to laugh in community. It is the connective force that reminds us how freeing it feels to just be. When we laugh, we are deeply present. This is what makes it a soulful experience. We are not thinking about yesterday or worrying about tomorrow; we are here now, smiling.

DAY 219.

IF YOU ARE A BUSYBODY OR OVERACHIEVER, DOING "NOTHING" IS PROBABLY THE GREATEST "SOMETHING" YOU COULD DO FOR YOURSELF.

* YOU ARE ALLOWED TO JUST BE. WE CANNOT ACTIVELY PRODUCE, EXERT, OR EVEN RECEIVE ENERGY EVERY SINGLE DAY. SOME DAYS WE NEED TO QUIETLY REST ON ZERO.

DAY 220.

Creativity is not limited to the arts. We are all creative. Yes, we create paintings, poems, songs, music, dance, and theater, but we also create communities, solutions, new ideas, policies, spreadsheets, laughter, even people! Creativity is the voice within that says *there could be something more here*. It connects us to hope and reminds us that one of the things people are best at creating is . . . change.

DAY 221.

THE CATERPILLAR WANTS TO STAY SAFE, IN THE COCOON IT KNOWS SO WELL, BUT TO LET IT FALL AWAY IS TO FLY.

Are things falling apart or falling away? Life consistently asks us to shed. We shed relationships, jobs, roles, interests, and phases of life. These transitions may feel uncomfortable or sad in the moment, but they are often the only way to get to what's next.

DAY 222.

Grief comes in many forms. We lose parts of ourselves that we never get back, relationships end, dreams expire, and feelings fade. Know that if you feel lost in your loss, it will not last forever. When we have been in a foreign space for long enough, we begin to make a map. We begin the search for something new. Beginnings follow endings, eventually.

DAY 223.

"The most powerful healing arises from the simple intention to love the life within you, unconditionally, with as much tenderness and presence as possible."

—Tara Brach

The love within you is your home. It is warm, welcoming, and waiting to receive us no matter how far away we have drifted.

DAY 224.

WE ARE ALL DIVINE AND HERE ON PURPOSE. NO ONE IS A MISTAKE. THOUGH LIFE MAY HARDEN AND CORRUPT THE SOULS OF SOME, KNOW THAT WE ALL BEGIN WITH LIGHT AND GOODNESS. NO ONE IS BORN "BAD." MAY THIS TRUTH FILL US WITH THE GRACE AND MERCY SO MANY NEED TODAY.

DAY 225.

Belonging is essential to human happiness. We must seek it, provide it, and be open to it. We endlessly benefit from contributing to and being supported by a kind, loving, and safe community. The lone wolf mentality may seem strong, but it often leads to anger, sadness, resentment, and disillusionment. In today's world, it is all too easy to isolate, but we must get outside and get involved. Connection to others brings a sense of purpose to our daily lives.

DAY 226.

TO LIVE IS TO GET LOST. THE SHIMMERY, MAGICAL PART OF THIS INEVITABILITY IS THE REUNION. THE POWER TO EMBRACE YOURSELF TIME AND TIME AGAIN. YOU ARE ALWAYS WELCOME IN THE HOME YOU HAVE WITHIN.

DAY 227.

When Bob Marley used the phrase "Lively Up Yourself," it meant to stir up the energy in our bodies. He would "lively up" himself by eating nourishing foods, connecting to spirit, moving his body, listening to music. In today's world, many of us wake up feeling tired and sluggish. His famous words remind us that we can combat those feelings, create vitality, feel alive, and seize the day.

DAY 228.

THE WORDS "I'M SORRY" HAVE THE POWER TO HEAL AND RECONNECT US IN MOMENTS OF FRACTURE. SELF-RIGHTEOUSNESS SEPARATES US; HUMILITY LINKS US. WE APOLOGIZE SO WE CAN MOVE FORWARD WITH EVERYONE INVOLVED FEELING SEEN AND UNDERSTOOD.

DAY 229.

We can only attract what we are truly open to. There are times we say we want certain things, but deep down, we have not removed the walls we unconsciously built between ourselves and our desires. For example, we might say we want to fall in love but our fear of intimacy causes us to continually choose noncommittal partners. True transformation flows when we are honest about what we are ready for and prioritize doing the inner work to welcome what's possible.

DAY 230.

You will invent and reinvent yourself many times if you're lucky. We are one body living one life, but within us are countless lives longing to roam free. Each one wants to dance, jump in the ocean, feel the sand beneath their feet, and taste the world. Staying the same does not serve you and ignoring hidden parts of yourself won't make them go away. Feeling aligned does not come from perfecting one way of being and sticking to it forever. It comes from walking your unique path.

DAY 231.

OUR DREAMS, ART, AND NEW IDEAS NEED INCUBATION PERIODS. LIKE IN COOKING, WHEN WE MARINATE SOMETHING, WE GIVE TIME FOR THE FULL FLAVOR TO SOAK IN BEFORE WE PUT IT IN THE OVEN.

DAY 232.

Self-doubt comes from consistently wrapping our goals and desires in negative thinking. Luckily, this is more of a habit than a permanent condition, and most habits can be changed. Just as most thoughts can be shifted, self-doubt can be dismissed, minimized, and replaced with more helpful ideas. If self-doubt says, *Why you?* your higher self can respond, *Why not me?* If it says, *You might fail*, your higher self can respond, *But I might succeed*. If it says, *You can't*, respond with, *What if I can?*

DAY 233.

TRUST THAT YOU KNOW WHAT IS RIGHT FOR YOU. EACH OF US HAS INNER WISDOM—A LOVING, DISCERNING VOICE WITHIN THAT WANTS THE BEST FOR US. LET IT GUIDE YOU TO THE PEOPLE AND SITUATIONS THAT HONOR WHO YOU ARE AND ALL YOU HAVE TO OFFER.

DAY 234.

We spend a big chunk of our lives waiting—in lines, for flights, on trains, and in traffic. We can spend that time feeling frustrated and impatient, or we can allow that time to be pleasant. Waiting can be an opportunity to soak in our thoughts, listen to music, call a loved one, notice the clouds, or even meet someone new. We cannot change the passage of time, but we can change our experience of it by choosing a good mood.

DAY 235.

a life in layers

we fall in love
we lose love
we leave the places we love
aliveness is beauty wrapped in pain wrapped in old souls wrapped in rebirth wrapped in tears, yearning, calamity, laughter, tragedy, and miracles.
aliveness is what happens now wrapped in what happens next wrapped in *tell me more* wrapped in *I don't know* wrapped in *no worries* wrapped in surrender, hello, goodbye, see you next time.

DAY 236.

WE CANNOT SHAME PEOPLE INTO CHANGE OR BULLY THEM OUT OF A POINT OF VIEW. IN MOMENTS OF DISAGREEMENT, WE CAN OWN OUR OPINIONS CONFIDENTLY WITH LOVING-KINDNESS RATHER THAN ATTACK THE OTHER. A CALM, STEADY FORCE USUALLY TAKES YOU MUCH FURTHER THAN A TUMULTUOUS ONE.

DAY 237.

Know your limits. Know how much you can do for others before your generosity turns into resentment. Service is important. Helping others is important. But these acts must flow with positive energy in order to be meaningful. None of us has an infinite supply of fuel. We have to pause and pour into ourselves in order to continuously give to others. Your needs are allowed to factor into your generosity. This is not selfish—it's realistic. To be a giver you must have something to give.

DAY 238.

Your ideas deserve to come to fruition, and that is only possible if you get to work. You have to be willing to do more than talk about your dreams. When you talk the talk for too long without walking the walk, you eventually exhaust everyone around you—including yourself. Action builds momentum. Start today—even if it's a small step.

DAY 239.

INSTEAD OF CREATING A BUBBLE THAT DENIES OR IGNORES THE PAIN, CHAOS, AND INJUSTICE IN OUR WORLD, CREATE A NEST—A WARM SAFE-SPACE TO PROCESS AND PROBLEM-SOLVE THESE REALITIES WITH YOUR LOVED ONES.

DAY 240.

Distance is not always avoidance. Sometimes, distance is the boundary we need to reflect, heal our hurt feelings, and avoid reinjury. Conflicts must be mended at a pace that works for all involved. It is always okay to pause and take the space you need to feel ready for repair.

DAY 241.

Flow is when our mind and body are in harmony. We can find it through dancing, rock climbing, cooking, walking in nature, or any activity that lives outside of worrying, calculating, strategizing, or competing with others. A flow state can calm your nervous system, shift your mood, and energize you when you feel sluggish.

DAY 242.

A NEW BEGINNING IS ALWAYS AVAILABLE TO US. WE ARE NOT TRAPPED IN OR BEHOLDEN TO OUTDATED VERSIONS OF OURSELVES OR OUR LIVES. WE GET TO CHOOSE CHANGE. WE GET TO CHOOSE AWAY FROM OUR PAST PATTERNS. WE GET TO LEAVE OUR GHOSTS IN THE SHADOWS AND WALK IN THE SUN WITH NEW FRIENDS.

DAY 243.

"Hope is the belief that our tomorrows can be better than our todays. Hope isn't magic, it is work."

—DeRay Mckesson

Hope is following your beliefs with your feet. When we want better, we work toward it.

DAY 244.

AN ARTIST IS ONLY AS TALENTED AS THE MEDIUM IN WHICH THEY FIND A SENSE OF HOME. GENIUS, LIKE A FLOWER, BLOOMS IN ITS OWN WAY, IN ITS OWN TIME, BASED ON ITS SOIL AND ELEMENTS.

DAY 245.

When you feel the urge to dance, sing at the top of your lungs, be silly, or do something just for fun, allow yourself that release. We all have an inner child who wants to play and explore the many colors of the world around us. When we reparent ourselves in ways that are too strict or serious, we stifle that joyous being. The child within you deserves to run wild—especially if these freedoms were not nurtured or available to you growing up.

DAY 246.

LIGHT IS THE SUN, A FIREFLY, A ROARING FLAME, AND THE FAINT FLICKER FROM A CANDLE IN THE WINDOW. IN EVERY FORM, IT IS A DIVINE OFFERING OF MAGIC AND WARMTH. LIGHT ILLUMINATES THE MYSTERY WITHIN AND AROUND US.

DAY 247.

**baby, you are the strongest flower that ever grew,
remember that when the weather changes**

These words are from *Heart Talk*. I have seen them painted on walls, collaged on graduation caps, and even tattooed on biceps. I think that is because, deep down, we know we have the strength to make it through whatever weather comes our way. We know that we are delicate *and* durable, like our favorite flower. We know that if we don't give up, we will make it through the storm, into the new day. Little reminders like this poem help us carry on in the rain.

DAY 248.

A friend once told me she manages her relationship to her phone by imagining herself physically disappearing from the room each time she picks it up. If this were true for you, how often would you vanish from your life? How much would you miss? As our phones and devices become more integrated into our daily living, we will need to create more boundaries. Reflect on your digital habits and find your digital boundaries. Your phone, social media, and any other device can have a place in your life, but certainly don't belong everywhere. You deserve to be truly present. Stay in the room.

DAY 249.

FOLLOW THE ENERGY OF NATURE. THE TREES ARE GROUNDED IN THEIR ROOTS AND STILL SHED, BEND, AND SWAY IN THE BREEZE. IT IS DIFFICULT TO ENJOY AND EMBRACE LIFE'S MYSTERY WHEN WE ARE TENSE AND RIGID. FLEXIBILITY KEEPS US OPEN, PRESENT, AND AT EASE.

DAY 250.

Can you close your eyes and imagine emptying your thoughts, like water pouring from a pitcher? Releasing the good, the bad, the complicated, the recurring—just letting it flow down and away from you. These small moments of letting go and starting over help us lighten up and reset our energy.

DAY 251.

ADVERSITY IS UNAVOIDABLE AND CAN EVEN BE HELPFUL. OUR CHALLENGES OFTEN REVEAL OUR POTENTIAL. THROUGH THEM, WE CAN LEARN OUR CAPACITY, DISCOVER OUR CREATIVE POWER, AND STRENGTHEN OUR PROBLEM-SOLVING MUSCLES.

DAY 252.

WHEN WE ARE MOVING THROUGH UNCOMFORTABLE FEELINGS LIKE ANXIETY, SADNESS, AND OVERWHELM, IT HELPS TO BELIEVE THERE IS AN "OKAY PLACE," A SPIRITUAL CENTER, FOR US TO RETURN TO. LIKE DOROTHY TRAVELING THROUGH OZ TO GET BACK TO KANSAS, WE, TOO, CAN MAKE IT HOME.

DAY 253.

When in disagreement with someone, especially a loved one, remember that everyone involved has feelings. Amid debates on moral, political, or other deeply personal ideas, our passion can sometimes lead us to speak to others in ways that are unkind and unhelpful. When we talk to someone as if they are not a breathing, feeling being, we diminish the fullness of their humanity. We can disagree with respectful feedback and boundaries. Doing so is the only way we get closer to any kind of resolution or repair.

DAY 254.

"The best way to take care of the future is to take care of the present moment."

—Thich Nhat Hanh

The future doesn't simply arrive one day; we are building it in every moment. Our words and actions today are creating what our world will look like tomorrow.

DAY 255.

A DEVOTION TO EARTH'S
BEAUTY AND MIRACLES
IS NOT A DENIAL OF ITS
PROBLEMS. IT IS A SWEET
AND POWERFUL REBELLION
AGAINST HOPELESSNESS.

DAY 256.

Notice how others respond when you stand up for yourself or set a boundary. Those who genuinely want the best for us are happy for us, not threatened by us, when we speak up and claim our needs. Stable, emotionally mature people want to be in a relationship where care and consideration go both ways.

DAY 257.

"Love challenges, be intrigued by mistakes, enjoy effort and keep on learning."

—Carol Dweck

Love is our great adventure and experiment. Just like any traveler or scientist, we must be open to what is revealed to us as we explore. We must remain curious and be willing to adapt to shifting terrain. The learning never ends. The trying never ends. Great love requires great ambition and endurance.

DAY 258.

OUR GUT INSTINCT IS SPIRIT TALKING. OUR NERVOUS SYSTEM IS OUR BODY TALKING. WE MUST NEVER UNDERESTIMATE THE WISDOM OUR BODIES HOLD. IT TELLS US WHEN TO STAY, WHEN TO GO, WHAT FEELS RIGHT, WHAT DOESN'T, WHO FEELS SAFE, AND WHO REQUIRES DISTANCE.

DAY 259.

When we continuously put our needs last, we create a dynamic where we must be small or nonexistent to fit in. We may think this is an act of generosity or benevolence toward our loved ones, but relationships that only serve one person eventually become too toxic to function. To sustain our relationships, we need shared care and responsibilities. Your needs are as important as everyone else's.

DAY 260.

"If you see someone without a smile today, give 'em yours."

—Dolly Parton

We all have a story about how someone's smile brightened our day. Many of us are drawn to people because of their laughs (dancing smiles). Smile today. It is the easiest way to add joy and beauty to your life.

DAY 261.

"The challenge is not to be perfect—it is to be whole."

—Jane Fonda

To be whole means you still have your heart and soul on the other side of your experiences—the victories and the despair. When this is the goal, we relax into the wisdom of our path.

DAY 262.

Finding a safe space is usually the first step in someone's healing journey. It is where they go with broken wings. It is where they go when they are lost and in need of direction or reinvention. Life can be so difficult; we must remember this when we encounter someone in need. It is an incredible gift to be a refuge for someone else.

DAY 263.

Your personal peace cannot be reliant on perfect conditions. We must be able to locate our calm and center no matter the chaos that surrounds us. You have the power to find security even on shaky ground.

DAY 264.

why not

take a break from being human
spend the afternoon as a wildflower
soaking up the water, basking in the sun, swaying,
  growing
smiling, probably
laughing, probably
dancing, probably

DAY 265.

OUR INSTINCTS ARE ANTENNAE PICKING UP SIGNALS AND INFORMATION ALL AROUND US. WHEN WE TUNE IN AND LISTEN TO OUR INNER GUIDANCE, IT TELLS US WHERE TO GO, WHAT TO DO, AND HOW IT DO IT IN A WAY THAT FEELS RIGHT FOR US.

DAY 266.

"It's not possible to constantly hold on to crisis. You have to have the love, and you have to have the magic. That's also life."

—Toni Morrison

We cannot bear the heaviness of our life's load every second of the day. We must create space to lighten up. Put down what is weighing on you, let your shoulders drop, and let something good hold you for a while. Receive this sweet relief.

DAY 267.

MEANINGFUL, LONG-TERM SOLUTIONS REQUIRE HEART. WHEN WE ATTEMPT TO SOLVE A PROBLEM WITHOUT LOVE, WE USUALLY END UP ADDING TO IT OR PUTTING A BAND-AID ON IT. LOVE WILL NEVER PATCH UP A WOUND; IT IS A REHABILITATING FORCE. IT HEALS FROM TOP TO BOTTOM, FROM THE INSIDE OUT.

DAY 268.

EVERYONE IN OUR LIVES NEEDS SPACE TO BLOOM WITHOUT FEAR THAT THEIR GROWTH WILL MAKE US FEEL THREATENED OR ABANDONED. PART OF FEELING SAFE IN A RELATIONSHIP COMES FROM TRUST AND FREEDOM. LOVING SOMEONE MEANS SUPPORTING THEM AS THEY CHANGE. LOVE, LIFE, AND OUR BONDS MUST EVOLVE TOGETHER.

DAY 269.

Tradition and ritual bring a spiritual structure to the time we spend with our friends and family. Close-knit communities need accountability and containers for our togetherness. Whether you adopt past traditions or create new ones, know that it is in those moments that many of our best memories are made.

DAY 270.

We do not need to indulge in every thought that comes up, especially those that are negative and irrelevant. Thoughts cannot be given free rein to roam endlessly, in every direction of your mind. When we set internal boundaries, we can pause or redirect our thought flow. In doing so, we protect our peace and streamline our inner life. We have the power to invest in positive thoughts and say "no, thank you" to low-level energy and ideas that do not serve us.

DAY 271.

WE CANNOT STAY IN PLACES WE HAVE OUTGROWN. OUR COMFORT ZONES BECOME UNCOMFORTABLE WHEN WE STAY IN THEM TOO LONG. WE ARE BUILT TO STRETCH, TAKE RISKS, AND EMBRACE NEWNESS. WHEN YOUR ROOTS ARE BREAKING THE SOIL, DO NOT BE AFRAID TO REACH FOR THE SUN.

DAY 272.

PERSISTENCE BELIEVES IN RIGHT NOW AND TOMORROW. IT ENCOURAGES US TO SPEAK UP, ASK FOR WHAT WE NEED, AND TRY AGAIN WHEN WE FACE SETBACKS. PERSISTENCE REMINDS US WE CAN REACH OUR FINISH LINE, EVEN WHEN WE CAN'T SEE IT. WE JUST HAVE TO KEEP GOING.

DAY 273.

We don't have to go it alone. We can invite community into our big undertakings. If we have a unique or intense job, we can find people who share similar levels of responsibility. If we are raising kids, we can remember that parenting is group work—more than a one- or two-parent system—teachers, coaches, caregivers, friends, and family can all be part of our support network. If we want to run a marathon, we can link up with other runners. Want to learn to cook? Join a cooking club or host a potluck. Seek community. Togetherness will always make big tasks feel less overwhelming.

DAY 274.

"It's strange to be here. The mystery never leaves you alone."

—John O'Donohue

Our aliveness is a giant mystery, one we are not meant to solve. We are meant to live in it and flow with it, like a river moving toward an unknown sea. This idea can feel a little unnerving. We want to control; we want to know what happens next. But when we lean into the mystery by accepting its ever-presence, we can find okay-ness in not knowing. There is joy and wisdom to be found in this divine investigation.

DAY 275.

RESILIENCE IS THE UNDERSTANDING THAT ON THE OTHER SIDE OF STRESS, STRAIN, OR EVEN DISASTER, OUR HEARTS REMAIN TENDER AND DURABLE. BEATING. BREATHING. INFORMED. TRANSFORMED. STILL HERE. THERE IS WISDOM AND LIFE AFTER OUR STORMS.

DAY 276.

"Pain is an event, an experience that must be recognized, named and then used in some way in order for the experience to change, to be transformed into something else, strength or knowledge or action."

—Audre Lorde

Once we understand that pain does not hold the same shape within us forever, we can begin moving through it and molding it into something else. Allowing it and us to change and shift.

DAY 277.

WHAT DO YOU HOLD SACRED? FAMILY? FRIENDSHIP? LAUGHTER? KINDNESS? GENEROSITY? SERVICE? THE SAFETY OF CHILDREN? RESPECT FOR ELDERS? A DIVINE LIFE BELONGS TO THOSE WHO FOSTER IT.

DAY 278.

“There are years that ask questions and years that answer.”

—Zora Neale Hurston

A few years ago, I stopped believing in writer’s block. Now, I see those quiet periods as a sign to read, listen, and take things in. There are days, months, and years that wrap us in stillness and ask us to receive. Others push us into action and radical change. There is wisdom in all of it. Do not be afraid to go with life’s natural ebb and flow.

DAY 279.

FAST DOES NOT NECESSARILY MEAN BETTER. THE WORLD MAY REWARD THE QUICKNESS OF HUSTLE AND GRIND CULTURE, BUT YOU ARE ALLOWED TO MOVE FORWARD WITH GENTLE, SLOW INTENTION. LIFE IS ALLOWED TO BE UNHURRIED. AND WE OFTEN GET MORE OUT OF IT WHEN IT IS.

DAY 280.

WE ALL FACE THE TEMPTATION OF LETTING OUR LOWER ANGELS WALK US OUTSIDE OUR INTEGRITY. BUT WHEN WE HOLD THE LINE, WE STAY CONNECTED TO OUR SOUL. WE SMILE WITH UNCOMPLICATED HEARTS. AND WE LIVE IN THE POWER OF OUR LIGHT.

DAY 281.

I am holding on, but my hands are tired and turning red. This had me thinking, maybe love is about letting go instead.

We live with so much pent up and held in—our fists are clenched, our shoulders are tense, our breath is held. Let it go. And let it out. Lay down your burdens, especially if you have been carrying them too long. Release is a part of love. Love is a rhythm—holding on, letting go, breathing in, breathing out. Find the tempo that feels good to you.

DAY 282.

RAIN OR SHINE, KINDNESS BELONGS.

It is easy to be kind when we are in a good mood and things are going our way. But what is the quality of our kindness amid disagreement, frustration, and exhaustion? We see how much we value kindness when our patience is tested. When struggling, take a deep breath and repeat the words, *I believe kindness belongs here.*

DAY 283.

VULNERABILITY IS A LIBERATING FORCE. WE STOP HIDING. WE STOP PRETENDING. WE SPEAK OUR TRUTH. WE GET RELIEF. WE GET SUPPORT. WE GET FREE.

DAY 284.

"Practice any art, music, singing, dancing, acting, drawing, painting, sculpting, poetry, fiction, essays, reportage, no matter how well or badly, not to get money and fame, but to experience becoming, to find out what's inside you, to make your soul grow."

—Kurt Vonnegut

Imagination and creativity have no expiration date. These gifts are lifelong gifts.

DAY 285.

Love requires witnessing. When we observe our loved ones with sweet curiosity and lightness instead of judgment and emotional strategizing, they feel free to fully be themselves. The power of listening and simply *being* with someone cannot be underestimated. It is to offer true beloved company in a world that too often feels too lonely to bear.

DAY 286.

Sometimes we must put ourselves through something over and over again until we can receive the lesson. Forgive yourself for this. We connect with others based on where we are healed *and* unhealed. Sometimes it is on the other side of our toxic relationships that we find the starting point for needed change and personal growth. Rock bottom can be the place we build a new, healthier foundation for ourselves. You are not alone. We have all been there. And when you are ready, whether it is on your own, or with the help of others, the lesson will land, and the last time will be the last time.

DAY 287.

TO BE HUMBLE IS TO BE DIVINE. HUMILITY KEEPS US CONNECTED TO OURSELVES AND OUR LOVED ONES. IN MOMENTS OF CELEBRATION, CONFLICT, AND IN THE AFTERMATH OF OUR MISTAKES.

DAY 288.

I RECENTLY SAW A PHOTOGRAPHY SERIES OF BEES NAPPING INSIDE FLOWERS. WE ALL STRUGGLE TO CLAIM MOMENTS OF REST AND RELAXATION. BUT IF EVEN THE BUSY BEE CAN TAKE TIME TO JUST BE (PUN INTENDED), HOW COULD WE POSSIBLY THINK WE ARE MEANT TO CONSTANTLY BE ON THE GO?

DAY 289.

The small stuff *is* the big stuff. We remember people not only from their great heroic gestures but from their little offerings—saying hello every time they see us, checking in on us and our family, letting us know when they are thinking of us. Seemingly insignificant deeds cannot be underestimated. Every piece of trash we pick up in our neighborhood is meaningful. Every dollar we give to someone in need helps. Every person we pray for or send a blessing is important. Small, simple acts of kindness can be life-changing and world changing.

DAY 290.

Failure is not a home; it is a teacher. We do not live in it; we learn from it. The lessons can be tough and unpleasant, but they can also be instructive. There is wisdom to be found in both our positive and negative outcomes. Getting it wrong can lead us to dive deeper into ourselves and our creative wells. Let failure inform you as you move forward, not keep you from moving forward.

DAY 291.

WHEN WE TRY TO AVOID FEAR, WE OFTEN GIVE IT EXTRA POWER AND CONTROL OVER OUR LIVES. INSTEAD OF TRYING TO GET RID OF IT, WE CAN FOCUS ON GIVING IT A PROPER PLACE. LET FEAR LIVE AS A QUIET VOICE IN THE BACK OF YOUR HEAD. JUST BECAUSE YOU CAN HEAR IT DOES NOT MEAN YOU HAVE TO LISTEN TO IT.

DAY 292.

NO ONE HAS THE POWER TO TELL YOU WHO YOU ARE. EVEN OUR MOST LOVED FRIENDS AND FAMILY CAN PROJECT STORIES AND IDENTITIES ONTO US THAT DO NOT FEEL RIGHT OR TRUE. YOUR LIFE STORY IS YOURS TO CLAIM, RECLAIM, SHARE, CHANGE, SHIFT, AND PROTECT.

DAY 293.

If we want to live in a beloved community, the very least we can do is learn how to control our tone. Maybe we can't avoid feeling annoyed or agitated by others, but we are very much in control of how we speak to people. In fact, how we speak to people is usually how we are remembered. When our bad days or less-than-perfect experiences lead us to speak to others with rudeness or cruelty, it leaves an impression. Likewise, we never forget the people who maintain kindness and calm in the face of an inconvenience or unpleasant circumstances.

DAY 294.

YOUR BOUNDARIES TEACH OTHERS HOW TO HANDLE YOU WITH CARE.

What if we saw boundaries as our personal operating instructions—a set of guidelines that help others understand how to interact with us? If someone read your emotional manual, what would it say? What makes you feel seen and safe in a relationship? What behaviors feel functional? What don't? Many of us struggle to communicate our boundaries because we've never taken the time to define them for ourselves.

DAY 295.

WHEN A WEBSITE ASKS US TO CHECK THE BOX THAT SAYS "I AM NOT A ROBOT," LET'S TAKE THAT MANTRA WITH US INTO OUR DAY. SLOW DOWN. THE PACE OF A MACHINE WILL NEVER BE YOUR PACE. WE ARE NOT BUILT TO MOVE AT THE SPEED OF OUR WI-FI.

DAY 296.

Life is a series of transitions. Like a seed moving through the seasons, we become one with the natural world. We sprout, we bloom, we enjoy our time in the sun and return to the earth. Accepting these inevitabilities allows us to flow with the rhythm of aliveness. We can relax into our shifts rather than problematize them. A tree does not feel there is something wrong when its leaves begin to shed. It instead smiles at the cool breeze and says hello to fall.

DAY 297.

Know what you like. Doing things we don't enjoy often puts us on edge, we can't fully relax, and it is hard to connect with others. We can be flexible, we can try new things, and we can endure a little discomfort in those pursuits, but we must also be able to express our wants and give people a chance to experience us in our "happy place." Start by knowing where it is located.

DAY 298.

IT IS NATURAL TO FALL INTO JUDGMENT, BUT IT IS UNHELPFUL TO STAY THERE. LIMIT HOW MUCH TIME YOU GIVE IT. MOVE ON, TURN IT INTO COMPASSION, SEEK RESOLUTION, OR GET OVER IT.

DAY 299.

Before we enter a situation, we must remember that we are responsible for the energy we bring to it. If we don't feel like we can contribute positively, we can opt out, shift our mindset, or seek support. To attract positive people and a fun environment, we must bring that energy. Energy, like water, seeks its own level.

DAY 300.

IF ALL YOUR DREAMS CAME TRUE, WOULD THEY CHANGE JUST YOU OR WOULD THEY CHANGE THE WORLD?

Too many dreamers achieve their goals but lose their sense of purpose because their dreams were not bigger than themselves. We cannot only want from our world; we must give to it as well. Fulfillment does not come solely from our accolades; it comes from the depth of our service and connection to others.

DAY 301.

Our personal space is our garden. Everyone and everything around us contribute to the health of our soil. When we are surrounded by clutter, it is difficult to live with clarity. When we hang around people who do not encourage, comfort, or inspire us, it is difficult to grow. When our private life is sweet and stable, we can offer more patience and care in our public spaces. The more you tend to your own garden, the more you can contribute to the world around you.

DAY 302.

LOVE REMOVES DOUBT AND INSECURITY. WHEN WE LOVE OURSELVES THOROUGHLY, WE CAN REST INSTEAD OF CHASE. WE ARE AT EASE. WHEN WE LOVE OTHERS THOROUGHLY, OUR BELOVEDS DO NOT HAVE TO WONDER HOW WE FEEL ABOUT THEM. OUR WORDS AND ACTIONS MAKE IT KNOWN. THEY FEEL AT EASE.

DAY 303.

There are three words I always associate with my father: *Take your time.* It has been his answer to everything from challenging homework to heartbreak to walking in heels. Slowing down is often the best thing we can do for ourselves. When we feel panicked, scared, overwhelmed, or stressed, we do not need to accelerate. We can take it slow. We can take our time.

DAY 304.

IT IS NOT EGOTISTIC TO ACKNOWLEDGE YOUR GIFTS. WHEN WE KNOW WHAT WE ARE NATURALLY GOOD AT, WE CAN SHARE IT WITH CONFIDENCE AND IN ABUNDANCE. WHAT MAKES YOU SPECIAL IS YOUR GIFT TO HAVE AND YOUR GIFT TO GIVE TO OTHERS.

DAY 305.

Surrender is freedom. It is freedom from the energy of control, freedom from constantly strategizing to satisfy our wants, needs, and desires. Surrender comes up in most meditations because, in this state, we relax our body and mind. We do not need to be "on" or worried about what happens next. Surrender melts and mellows this tension. A mind at ease is better prepared to respond to what happens next.

DAY 306.

IF WE DID NOT KNOW
DARKNESS, WE WOULDN'T
HAVE DISCOVERED OUR DIVINE
ABILITY TO CREATE AND SHARE
LIGHT. MAGIC, STRENGTH,
AND BRAVERY ARE OFTEN
BORN FROM THE OCCASIONS
WE HAD TO RISE TO.

DAY 307.

Self-care is not one thing. It is a toolbox holding the many tools that help us feel good about ourselves and our decisions. It can include favorite people, life-affirming movement and food, soulful experiences, intimate time alone, books, songs, art, stillness, silliness, honesty, service, sun, and the sea. Create yours based on your unique needs.

DAY 308.

Collaboration is needed in art, relationships, community spaces, and work. The more we collaborate, the better we become at it. The more we value it, the more frequently we do it. Going it alone is a habit we choose. Collaboration is also a habit we choose. Only one of them is sustainable. As the African proverb goes, *If you want to go fast, go alone; if you want to go far, go together.*

DAY 309.

MANTRA FOR OVERWHELM:

ONE BREATH AT A TIME

ONE STEP AT A TIME

THE TOP OF THIS MOUNTAIN

DOESN'T MATTER RIGHT NOW.

DAY 310.

A militant devotion to structure can leave us feeling uptight and unfree. To be human is to explore and improvise. Newness and variety add zest to our lives—whether it be reading about something new, spending time with a new person, or even trying a new hobby. If we are too married to planning, we lose our relationship with discovery.

DAY 311.

DON'T TRY TO BULLY YOURSELF OUT OF A TOUGH MOMENT. OUR STRUGGLES DON'T NEED A DRILL SERGEANT, THEY NEED A MOTHER'S LOVE. GENTLE, NURTURING, HOLDS US UP, HOLDS US CLOSE, AND CARRIES US FORWARD WHEN WE FEEL DOWN AND OUT.

DAY 312.

Even when we must intentionally distance ourselves from someone because the relationship was damaging or dysfunctional, we may still miss them. Know that this is okay and normal. It may be a sign that you want to repair the relationship, or it may be a passing feeling that doesn't require action. Many relationships end while our feelings or attachments are still active. In these moments, it can be helpful to wish them well in your mind and move on. Doing this keeps us from falling back into situations that do not serve us.

DAY 313.

DO WHAT FEELS RIGHT FOR YOU WHEN IT FEELS RIGHT FOR YOU. DON'T LET ANYONE MAKE YOU FEEL YOU ARE BEHIND BECAUSE OF AGE, PHASE OF LIFE, OR ANYTHING ELSE. AS MARY OLIVER SAID, "THINGS TAKE THE TIME THEY TAKE." YOUR LIFE IS YOURS TO LIVE. YOUR PACE IS YOURS TO SET.

DAY 314.

Tara Brach once shared a story about a successful businessperson who was asked how to be successful. They replied, "Make good decisions." When asked how to make good decisions, they said, "Experience." Then they were asked, "How do you get experience?" They answered, "By making bad decisions." I love this story because it reminds us that if we keep shame at bay, we have the power to turn our mistakes into wisdom.

DAY 315.

Get excited for your loved ones. Make a big deal out of their accomplishments. Maybe they finished writing the first page of their book or maybe they finished writing the last page, got a promotion, or got through another tough week. Maybe they discovered something new—a band, book, hobby, or person. Offering supportive, joyful, upbeat energy reminds them that they are seen, important, and celebrated.

DAY 316.

Part of being understood is making yourself understood. It is unfair to think anyone around us can read our minds or know us better than we know ourselves. When we clearly communicate, it leaves less space for others to assume, worry about, or misinterpret what we are going through.

DAY 317.

CAN WE BE GRATEFUL FOR WHAT IS HERE AND HOW FAR WE HAVE COME? THROUGH PRESENCE AND GRATITUDE, WE CAN SETTLE INTO SATISFACTION. WE DO NOT NEED TO WAIT FOR TOMORROW. WE DO NOT NEED TO ACCOMPLISH ONE MORE THING. WE ARE WORTHY TODAY, RIGHT NOW.

DAY 318.

Accountability is often the extra push we need to overcome procrastination. When we create a community that checks in on and cares about our goals, it can help us begin or motivate us to move forward when we feel stuck.

DAY 319.

"As long as you're dancing, you can break the rules. Sometimes breaking the rules is just extending the rules. Sometimes there are no rules."

—Mary Oliver

We are allowed to follow more than just the rules. We are allowed to follow joy, freedom, and our hearts.

DAY 320.

We can always find a reason to not do our work. There will always be laundry to do, dishes that need washing, a random thing to look up online, a phone call to make, or a need of someone else's to tend to. Procrastination is a slippery force that shows up no matter who you are and what you do. To create, we must start our work and stay in our work.

DAY 321.

WE DON'T NEED TO OVERTHINK EVERYTHING. THERE ARE SOME THINGS WE CAN UNDERTHINK: GOSSIP, OUR LOOKS, OTHER PEOPLE'S LOOKS, CLUMSY MOMENTS, TRENDS, OR THAT TIME WE SAID THE WRONG THING. KNOW WHAT'S IMPORTANT AND LET GO OF THE REST.

DAY 322.

THERE ARE SOME THINGS WE NEVER GET OVER. THEY STAY WITH US AS WE GO ON.

When we understand that not all experiences can be left in the past or skipped over, we are better able to carry them when they show up in the present moment. When we have loved and lost someone, we do not simply move on. When we have been harmed or had our heart broken, we cannot merely "get over it." We live with, work with, and heal alongside these experiences.

DAY 323.

LOVE ADDS "RIGHT NOW"

TO OUR STRUGGLES.

I AM LOST RIGHT NOW

I AM SAD RIGHT NOW

I AM ANXIOUS RIGHT NOW

* SELF-LOVE REMINDS US THAT A LOW MOMENT IS A MOMENT, NOT A PERMANENT STATE.

DAY 324.

“If it doesn’t matter in five years, it doesn’t matter.”

—Cher

Our daily lives are filled with little dramas that distract us from our goals and drain our energy. Know when to keep it moving. Much of what emotionally inflames us fades into irrelevancy faster than we think.

DAY 325.

Yes is a giant, life-changing energy. Having open, welcoming energy is a deliberate choice. We nurture it with a commitment to curiosity and possibility. Fear of disappointment can block our ability to say yes to and work toward what we want. Know that you are worthy of the opportunities that lead you to where you want to go. It all starts with saying yes.

DAY 326.

When we have a personal ethos, we know who we are and what we stand for. If we believe in nonviolence, we will never think the solution to violence is more violence, whether that be a schoolyard fight or an endless war. If we believe in telling the truth, we will not accept lies. If we believe in basic goodness, we will not accept cruelty. If we believe in democracy, it is easy to identify what and who threatens it. When we are firmly rooted in our moral center, we make better choices for ourselves because we are clear on what is right or wrong.

DAY 327.

FROM CHILDHOOD TO OLD AGE. WE NEED A HAND TO HOLD AND A KIND VOICE ENCOURAGING US TO TRY, LOVE, AND BELIEVE. WHEN WE HAVE SWEET, SUPPORTIVE COMPANIONSHIP IN EVERY PHASE OF LIFE, WE HAVE A SOFT PLACE TO LAND WHENEVER WE FALL.

DAY 328.

Only the negative words you believe about yourself can hurt you. It never feels good to hear something hurtful or untrue, but gossip, lies, and unkind opinions cannot cause real, long-term harm unless we internalize them. Sometimes we may need to face critique that makes us uncomfortable, but it is important to know what belongs to us and what doesn't. We do not have to be at the mercy of other people's judgments of us. As a friend of mine likes to say, "What other people think of me is none of my business."

DAY 329.

Most long-lasting relationships are formed over bonds of character. Our interests and lifestyles may change, but when we share core values with our partner, friends, and family, we are linked in a larger, deeper, more sustainable way. These connections strengthen us in times of need and are usually the ones that lead us back to ourselves when we feel lost.

DAY 330.

"Everyone is a genius, but if you judge a fish by its ability to climb a tree, it will live its whole life believing it is stupid."

—Albert Einstein

Many of us struggle to find confidence or purpose because we are trying to squeeze ourselves into shoes that don't fit.

DAY 331.

HAPPINESS OFTEN BEGINS WITH WHAT YOU ALLOW YOURSELF TO HAVE. WILL YOU LET YOURSELF HAVE GOOD LOVE? WILL YOU LET YOURSELF BE SURROUNDED BY PEOPLE WHO UPLIFT AND COMFORT YOU? WILL YOU LET YOURSELF BE THE MAIN CHARACTER IN YOUR LIFE? ARE YOU READY TO PUT YOURSELF FIRST?

DAY 332.

"Your playing small doesn't serve the world."

—Marianne Williamson

When we shrink or play it small, we not only diminish the value of our own self-worth, we also limit how much we can help others. What we give to the world creates a ripple long after we have gone. How big will you make yours?

DAY 333.

EACH OF US IS A BALL OF CONTRADICTIONS. WE NEED INDEPENDENCE AND BELONGING, JUNK AND TREASURES, LAUGHTER AND TEARS, THE DEEP END AND THE SHALLOW END. ALL THIS LIVES INSIDE OF US AND EXISTS IN THE WORLD AROUND US.

DAY 334.

Sometimes we follow recommendations from media or "gurus" that don't make us feel good or relaxed. They may even harm our self-esteem and further complicate our relationship with food and our bodies. We are free to make our own rules around what feels right. Maybe yoga feels like work and bowling feels like wellness. Maybe going to the museum feels more grounding than meditation. There is no one way to feed our mind-body connection.

DAY 335.

When someone has triggered us or caused us harm, we may feel a primal urge to to retaliate or seek revenge. But our spiritual self knows that causing destruction hardens our hearts and muddies our conscience. We will always sleep better at night knowing we chose kindness, even when cruelty felt justified. We do not need to teach anyone a lesson; the universe does that. Our job is to keep our own lives as sweet and soulful as possible.

DAY 336.

We are complex and ever-changing. When our emotions, relationships, or circumstances shift, it is natural to rethink what we want. Our old goals can become outdated, irrelevant, or at odds with new wants, desires, and interests. Allow yourself to reset your goals as you evolve.

DAY 337.

KINDNESS ALWAYS BELONGS. THE LAST THING YOU OR ANYONE AROUND YOU NEEDS IS ANOTHER SHARP EDGE. WE CAN SOFTEN. AND IN OUR SOFTNESS, WE CAN STILL BE DELIBERATE, BRAVE, AND PRINCIPLED.

DAY 338.

YOU DON'T HAVE TO BELIEVE EVERYTHING YOU THINK. NOT EVERY THOUGHT IS TRUE OR HELPFUL. OUR THOUGHTS REQUIRE REFLECTION, GUIDANCE, AND FILTRATION TO BE USEFUL, MEANINGFUL, AND POWERFUL.

DAY 339.

IMAGINE WHAT YOU COULD DO IF YOU DID SOMETHING ABOUT ALL YOU IMAGINE.

Discipline is often what separates the dreamers from the doers. We all have brilliant ideas. We all have something special that the world deserves to receive. If you want to be a writer, you must sit down and write. If you want to be a singer, you must sing a song. Make the thing, cook the thing, start the thing. Discipline transforms our ideas into offerings.

DAY 340.

SOME DAYS, THE BEST WE CAN FEEL IS OKAY. AND THAT IS . . . OKAY. IT ISN'T ALWAYS POSSIBLE TO QUICKLY SHIFT FROM MELANCHOLY TO OVERJOYED. FINDING "OKAY" IS AN IMPORTANT STEP ON OUR EMOTIONAL LADDER AND A SAFE PLACE TO REST WHEN FEELING GOOD FEELS FAR AWAY.

DAY 341.

"If I can't dance, it is not my revolution."

—Emma Goldman

There will always be work for us to do to make our communities more just and loving. Even when our mission is serious, we need moments that energize us and remind us of what we are working toward. Life's little delights are a fueling force.

DAY 342.

We don't have to accept the roles people demand from us. Just because we are good at cleaning up messes doesn't mean we must play the role of the emotional janitor. Just because we are responsible doesn't mean we must always take on the role of the unfun parent. Just because we are organized doesn't mean we must oversee the planning every time. We can decide how we show up in our relationships. Part of being an adult is letting other adults be adults too. Just because something is within our capacity does not make it our responsibility.

DAY 343.

Make wishes—on your birthday, when the clock strikes 11:11, and when you see a shooting star. As we get older, we lose touch with the act of wishing, but it is a beautiful opportunity for an intentional pause. Wishing invites an intimate, hopeful dialogue within. Don't skip the chance to wish. If you never make a wish, how do you know if it will ever come true?

DAY 344.

—

I SAID TO THE ROAD,

"WHERE DO YOU LEAD?"

THE ROAD SAID, "BE A

LEADER AND FIND OUT."

We cocreate our sacred path with the universe. There are no directions. There are no maps. Where we are meant to go reveals itself to us with every step we are willing to take.

DAY 345.

"When it's over, I want to say: all my life

I was a bride married to amazement."

—Mary Oliver

Do not underestimate the power of awe—to sit, see, feel, and take in life's magic.

DAY 346.

Slow-growing vegetables are often the most nutrient dense. They take longer but offer more. It is difficult to create something high quality when we are too focused on speed. Deep presence and care bring spiritual value to everything—whether it be our work, our relationships, or our lives as a whole.

DAY 347.

IN THE MIDST OF LIFE'S RESPONSIBILITIES, PLAY CAN FEEL LIKE A LUXURY WE CAN'T AFFORD. BUT THE PHYSICAL, MENTAL, AND SOCIAL BENEFITS OF PLAY ARE ENDLESS. FROM CARD GAMES TO PUZZLES TO PAINTING, PLAY ISN'T EXTRA—IT'S ESSENTIAL. IT INSPIRES US, RELIEVES STRESS, AND BRINGS JOY.

DAY 348.

Falling in love, chasing your dreams, choosing your family, none of the big stuff comes without risk. The sooner we accept this, the sooner we can take a deep breath and go for it. Maybe it works out, maybe it doesn't, but if you don't try, you will always wonder if the life you have is the one you want or the one you let be enough.

DAY 349.

Know how to work with your energy. When we know when to go full throttle, when to move at a low power mode, and when to shut down to recharge, we are more likely to avoid burnout. Listen to yourself. Understand your limits and know that what you have to give will change from day to day.

DAY 350.

Loyalty brings loving, secure energy to our relationships. But what are we asking our loved ones to be loyal to? Are we asking them to be loyal to our ego? To our need to be right? Are we asking them to take our side regardless of their own opinions and feelings? Spiritual loyalty is loving someone toward their highest good. It is a commitment to our current feelings and our future self. It is honest, kind, and fair, no matter the situation.

DAY 351.

IT IS ALWAYS OKAY TO NOT KNOW THE ANSWER, BUT IT SHOULDN'T BE BECAUSE WE DIDN'T HAVE THE COURAGE TO ASK THE QUESTION.

The more we investigate, the more we know and understand our world—the wrong and the right, the pain and the beauty. Seeking knowledge awakens and softens our hearts. It builds empathy, inspires generosity, and reaches for justice. If we want to know the full potential of our existence, we must remain curious, ask questions, and seek truth.

DAY 352.

There is a reason we cheer for teams at sporting events, for musicians at concerts, and for actors in the theater. It boosts their energy and confidence. Affirmation does the same for us in our personal lives. See just how much further you can go when you cheer yourself on.

DAY 353.

worthy, you

when you have stayed small for too long
there are three words you will never regret saying out loud
to yourself or
anyone else:
I deserve more

DAY 354.

The kindness we struggle to show others is the same kindness we deny ourselves within. Can you be kind to yourself in your mistakes or low moments? Is your self-talk kind? Do you believe that when you are at your worst, you deserve self-kindness? Kindness is how we remain soft and offer softness to the sharp corners of the world.

DAY 355.

Our differences add flavor to the world. The variety of ways people think, dress, look, speak, cook, laugh, dance, and sing is exciting and interesting. We do not need to be threatened by what we don't know; we can learn about it. Sameness is not safer; it is often duller and makes us more closed off. The opportunity to know and love people from all different backgrounds is an immense privilege. Earth's people are a magical part of the great mystery of life.

DAY 356.

what an offering

whenever you want to witness generosity
find a river
watch the way it flows with power and ease, creating neighbors and connecting unknown lands
see how freely it offers itself to all
a place to sit
a place to eat
a place to be

DAY 357.

WHAT WE WANT IS HELD IN THE SAME HANDS AS WHAT WE GIVE.

Reciprocity is mutual respect in motion. It is the connective force that honors each person's need to be seen and held. If we are good at giving, we must work on receiving. If we are good at receiving, we must work on giving. We need both energies for there to be a stable, peaceful flow.

DAY 358.

EMPATHY AND COMPASSION BRING HEAVEN TO EARTH. TO OFFER DEEP UNDERSTANDING AND LOVING-KINDNESS TO THE EXPERIENCE OF ANOTHER HUMAN BEING IS A DIVINE ACT. IT BRINGS PEACE TO PAIN. IT GATHERS THE PIECES OF A BROKEN HOME AND REBUILDS IT AS A TEMPLE.

DAY 359.

"Some people feel the rain. Others just get wet."

—Bob Dylan

How you frame your experiences dictates the quality of your life. We can view a rainy day as calamity or inconvenience or we can embrace it as a moment of freedom, a moment of surrender and calm, a moment to witness the breathtaking power of the earth's sky. We can choose awe. We can choose to feel. Or we can, as Bob Dylan says, just get wet.

DAY 360.

THE WISE DO NOT FORGET THAT NATURE IS A MOTHER.

The natural world is a maternal force that nurtures and nourishes us. We survive because of the light of her sun, the air she gifts from her plants, and the water she streams all around us. Our relationship with Earth can feel like the relationship between child and parent. We can be too consumed with our own youthful needs to consider the experiences of our elders. But with maturity comes gratitude. How can we say thank you? We give thanks to our planet, our parent, by respecting all she does for us.

DAY 361.

BELIEVE IN MAGICAL THINKING. BELIEVE IN MIRACLES. BELIEVE THAT CHANGE IS POSSIBLE. WE WILL ALWAYS HAVE TO WORK TOWARD A BETTER WORLD, BUT WE MUST NEVER UNDERESTIMATE THE POWER OF RELENTLESS HOPE. IT IS THE LIGHT WE HOLD WHEN WE MUST JOURNEY DOWN A LONG, DARK ROAD.

DAY 362.

a good inheritance

each of us
will leave a footprint here once we've gone
what will yours be in the shape of?
love?
justice?
hope?
freedom?
my goodness, what divine shoes to fill

DAY 363.

"Do not disturb yourself by imagining your whole life at once."

—Marcus Aurelius

One breath at a time. One step at a time. Everything that needs to get done will get done. Everything that shall be, shall be.

DAY 364.

"You can't go back and change the beginning, but you can start where you are and change the ending."

—C. S. Lewis

You are the artist and the masterpiece, the sculptor and the sculpture, the singer and the song, the writer and the story. The life you want is in your hands.

DAY 365.

new beginnings

we live
in a world
of
sunrises
if the earth is given a chance to start over every single
day, aren't you?

acknowledgments

To Raheal, Cait, and Shannon—thank you for the work and care you put into this book, for making it possible.

To Simon and our fun, funny family—thank you for all of the ways you inspire, support, and encourage everything that I make. I love you.

To my girlfriends, aka "the aunties," thank you for being there through the books, the kids, the new cities. All of it.

To my readers, thank you for being there. Us, always.

about the author

CLEO WADE is a #1 *New York Times* bestselling author, poet, and artist whose work explores hope, resilience, and the immense power of love. Born and raised in New Orleans, Louisiana, Cleo currently lives in California with her partner, Simon, and their three daughters, Memphis, Bayou, and Magnolia.

Also by Cleo Wade

Heart Talk: Poetic Wisdom for a Better Life

Where to Begin: A Small Book About Your Power to Create Big Change

Remember Love: Words for Tender Times

What the Road Said

May You Love and Be Loved: Wishes for Your Life

Avid Reader Press, an imprint of Simon & Schuster, is built on the idea that the most rewarding publishing has three common denominators: great books, published with intense focus, in true partnership. Thank you to the Avid Reader Press colleagues who collaborated on *In a World of Sunrises*, as well as to the hundreds of professionals in the Simon & Schuster advertising, audio, communications, design, ebook, finance, human resources, legal, marketing, operations, production, sales, supply chain, subsidiary rights, and warehouse departments whose invaluable support and expertise benefit every one of our titles.

Editorial
Shannon Welch, *VP and Editorial Director*
Megan Noes, *Editorial Assistant*

Jacket Design
Alison Forner, *Senior Art Director*
Clay Smith, *Senior Designer*
Sydney Newman, *Art Associate*

Marketing
Meredith Vilarello, *VP and Associate Publisher*
Caroline McGregor, *Senior Manager, Marketing*
Kayla Dee, *Associate Marketing Manager*
Katya Wiegmann, *Marketing and Publishing Assistant*

Production
Allison Green, *Managing Editor*
Hana Handzija, *Managing Editorial Assistant*
Jessica Chin, *Senior Manager of Copyediting*
Yvette Grant, *Senior Production Editor*
Alicia Brancato, *Production Manager*
Ruth Lee-Mui, *Interior Text Designer*
Cait Lamborne, *Ebook Developer*

Publicity
Alex Primiani, *Director Publicity*
Eva Kerins, *Publicity Assistant*

Subsidiary Rights
Paul O'Halloran, *VP and Director of Subsidiary Rights*
Fiona Sharp, *Subsidiary Rights Coordinator*